There is no "Elizabeth McNeill" — that is the pseudonym (for obvious reasons) of the New York career woman who experienced and wrote about the incredible nine and a half weeks that began with a casual encounter at a Manhattan street fair, and ended in a terrifying climax of bondage, humiliation and ecstasy. It is an experience from which she has never fully recovered; and which, she claims, she does not regret.

9½ WEEKS

"IT LEADS US TO THE EDGE OF THE ABYSS...WHERE THE BOUNDARIES OF SELF ARE OBLITERATED AND ALL THINGS BECOME PERMISSIBLE."

— *THE NEW YORK TIMES*

9½
WEEKS

A MEMOIR OF
A LOVE AFFAIR

BY ELIZABETH McNEILL

BERKLEY BOOKS, NEW YORK

Lyrics from "Me and Bobby McGee"
by Kris Kristofferson are quoted
with permission of Combine Music Corporation.

This Berkley book contains the complete
text of the original hardcover edition.
It has been completely reset in a typeface
designed for easy reading and was printed
from new film.

9½ WEEKS

A Berkley Book / published by arrangement with
E. P. Dutton

PRINTING HISTORY
Dutton edition published 1978
Berkley edition / February 1979

ISBN: 0-425-10384-6

A BERKLEY BOOK ® TM 757,375
Berkley Books are published by The Berkley Publishing Group,
200 Madison Avenue, New York, New York 10016.
The name "Berkley" and the "B" logo
are trademarks belonging to Berkley Publishing Corporation.

PRINTED IN THE UNITED STATES OF AMERICA

20   19   18   17   16   15   14   13

THE FIRST TIME we were in bed together he held my hands pinned down above my head. I liked it. I liked him. He was moody in a way that struck me as romantic; he was funny, bright, interesting to talk to; and he gave me pleasure.

The second time he picked my scarf up off the floor where I had dropped it while getting undressed, smiled, and said, "Would you let me blindfold you?" No one had blindfolded me in bed before and I liked it. I liked him even better than the first night and later couldn't stop smiling while brushing my teeth: I had found an extraordinarily skillful lover.

The third time he repeatedly brought me within a hairsbreadth of coming. When I was beside myself yet again and he stopped once more, I heard my voice, disembodied above the bed, pleading with him to continue. He obliged. I was beginning to fall in love.

The fourth time, when I was aroused enough

to be fairly oblivious, he used the same scarf to tie my wrists together. That morning, he had sent thirteen roses to my office.

IT'S SUNDAY, toward the end of May. I'm spending the afternoon with a friend of mine who left the company I work for over a year ago. To our mutual surprise we've been seeing more of each other during the intervening months than while we worked in the same office. She lives downtown and there is a street fair in her neighborhood. We've been walking and stopping and talking and eating and she has bought a battered and very pretty silver pillbox at one of the stalls selling old clothes, old books, odds and ends labeled "antique," and massive paintings of mournful women, acrylics encrusted at the corners of pink mouths.

I am trying to decide whether to backtrack half a block to the table where I've fingered a lace shawl that my friend has pronounced grubby. "It *was* grubby," I say loudly to her back, a little ahead of me, hoping to be heard above the din. "But can't you picture it washed and mended...." She looks back over her shoulder, cups her ear with her right hand, points at the woman in a very large man's suit who is perusing a set of drums with ardor; rolls her eyes, turns away. "Washed and repaired," I shout, "can't you see it washed? I think I should go back and buy it, it's got possibilities...." "Better do it, then," says a voice close to my left ear, "and soon, too. Somebody else will have bought and washed it before she hears you in this noise." I whisk around and give the man directly behind me an annoyed look, then face forward again and attempt to catch up with my friend. But I'm literally stuck. The mob has slowed down from a slow shuffle to no movement at all. Directly before me are three children under six, all with dripping Italian ices, the woman to my right waves a falafel with dangerous gusto, a guitarist has joined the drummer and their audience stands enthralled, immobile with food and fresh air and goodwill. "This is a street fair, the first of the season," says the voice at my left ear. "People get to talk to strangers, what would be the point, otherwise? I still think you should go back and get it, whatever it is."

The sun is bright, yet it's not hot at all, balmy; the sky gleams, air as clean as over a small town in Minnesota; the middle child ahead of me has just taken a lick from each of his friends' ices in turn, this is surely the loveliest of Sunday afternoons. "Just a mangy shawl," I say, "nothing much. Still, it's intricate handwork and only four dollars, the price of a movie, I guess I'll buy it after all." But now there is no place to go. We stand, facing each other, and smile. He is not wearing sunglasses and squints down at me; his hair falls across his forehead. His face turns attractive when he talks, even more so when he smiles; he probably takes lousy photos, I think, at least if he insists on being serious in front of a camera. He wears a frayed, pale pink shirt, rolled up at the sleeves; the khaki pants are baggy—not gay, anyway, I think; the way pants fit is one of the few remaining, if not always reliable, ways of telling—tennis shoes without socks. "I'll walk back with you," he says. "You won't lose your friend, the whole mess is only a couple of blocks long, you'll run into each other sooner or later unless she decides to give up on the whole area, of course." "She won't," I say. "She lives down here." He has begun shouldering his way back toward where we've come from and says, over his shoulder, "so do I. My name is..."

NOW IT'S THURSDAY. We ate out Sunday and Monday, at my apartment on Tuesday, Zabar's cold cuts at a party given by a colleague of mine on Wednesday. Tonight he is cooking dinner at his apartment. We are in the kitchen, talking while he makes a salad. He has refused my offers of help, has poured a glass of wine for each of us, and has just asked me if I have any brothers or sisters, when the phone rings. "Well, no," he says. "No, tonight's a bad night for me, really. No, I'm telling you, this shit can wait until tomorrow...." There is a long silence while he grimaces at me and shakes his head. Finally he explodes: "Oh, Christ! All *right*, come on over. But two hours, I swear, if you're not set in two hours, the hell with it, I've got plans for tonight...."

"This *dope*," he groans at me, disgruntled and sheepish. "I wish he'd get out of my life. He's a nice guy to have a beer with, but he's got nothing to do with me except he plays tennis at the same place and works for the same firm, where he keeps falling behind and then he needs a crash course on his homework, it's like junior high. He's not too smart and he's got no guts whatsoever. He's coming down at eight, same old thing, some stuff he should've done two weeks ago and now he's panicking. I'm really sorry. But we'll go in the bedroom and you can watch TV out here."

"I'd rather go home," I say. "No, you don't," he says. "Don't go home, that's just what I was afraid of. Look, we'll eat, you do something for a couple of hours, call your mother, whatever you feel like, and we'll still have a nice time after he leaves, it'll only be ten, O.K.?" "I don't usually call my mother when I've got to kill a couple of hours," I say. "I hate the idea of killing a couple of hours, period, I wish I had some work with me. . . ." "Take your pick," he says, "all you want, help yourself," holding his briefcase toward me eagerly, making me laugh.

"All right," I say. "I'll find something to read. But *I'll* go in the bedroom and I don't even want your friend to know that I'm here. If he's still here at ten I'll come out with a sheet over my head on a broom, making lewd gestures." "Great." He beams. "I'll take the TV in anyway, in case you get bored. And after dinner I'll run down to the newsstand on the next block and get you a bunch of magazines—

for looking up lewd gestures you might not think of on your own." "Thanks," I say, and he grins.

After salad and a steak, we drink coffee in the living room, sitting side by side on a deep couch covered in blue cotton faded almost into gray at the armrests and frayed along the piping. "What do you *do* to coffee," I ask. "Do," he repeats, perplexed, "nothing, it's done in a percolator, isn't it O.K.?" "Listen," I say, "I'll take a rain check on the magazines if you get me that Gide down, in the shiny white jacket, on the left top shelf in the dining room, the spine caught my eye at dinner. That man's always been plenty lewd for me." But when he pulls down the book it turns out to be in French. And the Kafka, which fell down when he dislodged the Gide, is in German. "Never mind," I say. "Would you have *Belinda's Heartbreak*? Better yet, how about *Passions of a Stormy Night*?" "I'm sorry," he says, "I don't believe I have either of those. . . ." His careful, uneasy tone of voice annoys me even more. "*War and Peace*, then," I say spitefully. "In that rare, exquisite Japanese translation."

He lays down the two books he has been holding and puts his arm around me. "Sweetheart . . ." "*And,*" I say, in a voice as petty and unpleasant as I feel, "it's a little premature, calling me sweetheart, isn't it? We've known each other for all of ninety-six hours." He draws me toward him and hugs me tightly. "Look, I can't tell you how sorry I am, this is a makeshift, a half-assed . . . I'll just call it off."

As soon as he turns toward the telephone I feel ridiculous. I clear my throat, swallow loudly, and say, "Forget it. It'll take me two hours just to read the paper, and if you'll give me some stationery I'll write a letter I've owed for months, it'll be a boost to my conscience. I'll need a pen, too."

He grins, relieved; walks over to a large oak desk at the other end of the living room, comes back with half an inch of fine, cream-colored paper; hands me the fountain pen from the inside pocket of his suit jacket, and lugs the TV into the bedroom. "I really hope you don't mind too much," he says. "This won't happen again." I cannot guess how thoroughly he will keep his promise.

By the time the intercom buzzes I'm settled on his bed, leaning into one of the pillows I've propped against the wall, my knees drawn up, his thick pen solid and comfortable in my hand. I hear two men greet each other, but once they begin talking steadily I can rarely make out separate words.

I write the letter (". . . met this man a few days ago, nice start, very different from Gerry, who's more than happy with Harriet these

days, you remember her...") take a cursory
glance at the *Times*, look at my horoscope in
the *Post*: "Theories are easily expounded,
discounted because everyone knows what they
are. Keep early hours clear for urgent pur-
chases." Just once in my life, I think, I'd like to
understand my horoscope. I stretch out my
legs, scrunch down on the pillow. During the
hours I've spent with him here I've paid little
attention to my surroundings. Now I find
there's not much to look at. It is a large, high-
ceilinged room, the floor covered with the same
gray carpet as the hallway and the living room.
The walls are white, completely bare. The
platform bed with its thin foam pallet is king-
size and appears small. The sheets are white—
fresh, I notice, as they were on Monday, how
often does this man change his sheets?—the
blanket pale gray, there is no bedspread. The
two tall windows in the wall to the left of the
bed are covered with bamboo shades, painted
white. On one side of the bed stands the chair
now holding the TV set; an end table of the
same wood as the platform flanks it on the
other side. The lamp on this table has a white
shade, a round, white and blue base—the kind
made from a Chinese vase—and a 75-watt
bulb. I'm glad for the graceful lamp base but I
think: wherever else he may do it, this man
clearly does not read his original-language

books in bed; why would anyone want to miss out on one of the most satisfying pleasures available? All he'd need is a better bulb, a few more pillows, and a reading lamp. . . .

I wonder what he thought of my bedroom. Less than half the size of this one, painted by myself and two women friends in an elusive pale peach, the precise shade of which I agonized over for close to three months. It had been worth it. I wonder what he thought of the flowered comforter, the matching curtains and sheets and pillow cases, the three tattered Greek throw rugs, the trinkets from each one of my trips crowding the surface of the chest, the makeup table, the bookshelves; the piles of junk mail and magazines and paperbacks heaped on the floor on either side of the bed, the three empty coffee mugs, the overflowing ashtrays, the Chinese takeout container— empty, but with a fork still stuck in it; the laundry stuffed into a pillowcase leaning in a corner; the newsprint photos of Al Pacino and Jack Nicholson stuck in the frame of the mirror above the table, along with a Polaroid of my broadly smiling parents and one of myself with a four-year-old cousin in Coney Island; and a postcard of Norwegian fjords, sent by a friend, and one of the Sicilian chapel I'd fallen in love with two years ago. And the framed *New Yorker* covers on the wall, and maps of all the countries I've been to, special cities circled in red; and my favorite: a stained menu in an ornate silver frame, Lüchow's, the first New York restaurant I'd ever been to, twelve years ago.

Now this room here, I say to myself, is too plain to be called plain. It's austere, if you want to be charitable, or chic, if you want to be snide, or boring, if you want to be honest. It is not, in any event, a room you'd call cozy. Hasn't anyone ever told him people put stuff on their walls? With his job he'd be able to afford some nice prints; and for the amount he must have paid for that monster of a Stella in the living room he could cover these walls in gold leaf....

The voices are louder now. It's almost nine o'clock. I get up off the bed, and walk past the tall chest of drawers with ornate brass handles and some scrollwork in the wood; a long, narrow Parsons-type table stands next to it, holding a twin to the lamp on the bedside table and stacks of professional journals. And there is the closet. It is wide, with two doors that meet in the middle. The right one creaks loudly when I pull them both open: I stand stock still, holding my breath. But the unseen stranger's voice has risen to almost a wail, while his purrs along, low and controlled. I feel like a sneak; as you should, I tell myself, that's just what you are.

Beyond the doors, the closet extends to the ceiling. There are two deep shelves above the clothes rack. From what I can tell—only the front edge of the top shelf is within my range of vision—it holds tan leather luggage, heavily scuffed; a camera case, ski boots, and three black vinyl folders labeled, across two-inch backs, "taxes." The shelf below houses five heavy, crew-neck sweaters: two dark blue, one black, one off-white, one maroon; and four stacks of shirts, every one either light blue, pale pink, or white. ("I call Brooks Brothers now, once a year," he will tell me, some days later. "They send me the shirts and I don't have to go there. I hate going in stores." When a shirt shows signs of fraying at the cuffs and collar, he keeps it in a separate pile and wears it at home, so I will learn; the man at the Chinese laundry returns the clean and pressed but frayed shirts bundled together, separated from the rest. If a shirt acquires a stain that cannot be removed he throws it out.)

Next to the shirts lie two tennis rackets, their handles protruding over the edge of the shelf. Six white polo shirts on cleaner's cardboard, five pairs of tennis shorts. (He plays on Tuesdays from 12:30 to 2:30, on Thursdays from 12:15 to 2, on Sundays from 3 to 5, year round, I will come to understand. He carries the rackets in the covers in which they came,

13

the rest of his gear in a brown paper bag.) Toward the right wall, still on the second shelf, sits a stack of ten white pillow cases, next to a larger one of ten white sheets.

Not counting the one he is presently wearing in the next room, and possibly others out to be cleaned, he owns nine suits. Three—dark gray, dark blue with pinstripes, gray tweed; all with vests, all cut identically—are brand new. Three others—white linen, medium gray flannel, blue and white seersucker; the first two with vests, and all, again, cut alike—barely less so. A gray gabardine and a dark gray wool with pinstripes may both be two years old; and there is a tuxedo. (It is four years old, he will later tell me; I will not see him wear it. He will mention at one point that his suits have been made by the same tailor in Little Italy for eleven years, and that he has not gone to a fitting for this year's or last year's suits, delighted to have persuaded the protesting tailor that it was unnecessary. "It suddenly dawned on me, why should I, year after year. It's such a drag and I've weighed the same since high school and I'm long past growing." When a suit shows any sign of wear he gives it to the Chinese man who does his laundry—though not the dry cleaning. "But he's a good two feet shorter than you," I will say when he disposes of the gray gabardine this way. "What can he possibly do with a suit of yours?" "Who knows," he says. "I never ask. He always takes them.")

He owns two pairs each of dark blue ski pants and old khakis, one with paint stains. ("I tried to do the bathroom a couple of years ago, some mistake. I'm no good at doing stuff I do just because I think I ought to. It's never worth it, that bathroom was the worst paint job you could hope to see.")

A beige raincoat hangs next to a dark wool overcoat, a down-filled ski jacket takes up a foot in width at the very end of the rack. A furled black umbrella leans in the left corner. Wedged diagonally across the back wall is a set of skis and poles. Suspended from a brass rod on the inside of the left door hang a dozen ties so similar that they seem like an expanse of one piece of fabric when I squint. Most are dark gray or dark blue with small, geometric patterns in maroon; two are dark blue with small white dots, the most adventurous is gray, discreetly patterned in white *and* maroon. ("I don't like variety in clothes," he will say. "My own clothes, I mean. I like to know that I'll look pretty much the same, day after day.") Lined up on the floor are three pairs of sneakers, four pairs of identical black, wing-tip shoes, one pair of plain, oxblood-colored loafers.

I shut the doors and tiptoe to the bureau

against the wall that divides the bedroom from the living room. It has six drawers: three shallow, two medium, the bottom one deep. I begin at the top. A stack of white, initialed handkerchiefs, a wristwatch without a watchband, an old pocket watch, a black silk bow tie folded once and—lying in the upturned lid of what might have been a jelly jar—one set of plain gold cuff links, one narrow gold tie clasp, and one made of dark blue enamel with a thin gold line running its length down the middle. Somebody gave that to him, I think, this is clearly a gift, a nice one, too. Next drawer: two pairs of black leather gloves, one lined, one not; a tan pair, unlined; large, puffy ski mittens; a cummerbund. Third: navy swimming trunks, a jockstrap, one pair of pajamas—navy with white piping—still in the manufacturer's plastic wrapping. Another gift? No, the price tag's still on it. The next drawer, first of the medium-sized ones, holds white jockey shorts, easily a couple of dozen. Fourteen pairs of white wool socks and a boiled-front shirt in cellophane are housed below. The largest drawer sticks and I have to tug at it repeatedly. When I've finally edged it open I stare in amazement: jammed to overflowing, the drawer bulges with what seem to be a thousand identical, long, black socks. I think: this man owns more socks than all the men I've ever known combined; what is he scared of, they'll shut down every knitting mill in the country overnight? ("I hate going to the laundry," he will say, a few weeks later. "It's simple once you figure it out but it took me long enough. The more of the stuff you keep around, the less often you have to go either to a laundry or to a store." I will watch him from the bed, my body liquid, afloat: he takes out two socks, pushes his hand into one—the skin shows through the weave at the heel, though there is, as yet, no sign of a hole—and drops the sock into the wastebasket. "It's better to have them all the same, too," he will tell me. "That way you never have to match them. I messed with that crap all through graduate school, it's a pain in the ass.")

I close the drawer, jump on the bed, lie on my back, bounce, ride a bicycle in the air above me. I'm beside myself. Falling in love with a stockpiler of socks, a sock-stockpiler, a man who socks away socks . . . I cannot keep from making grunting, snorting noises in my effort not to laugh out loud, though his slow friend's voice is piercing by now, I could probably shout "fire" without being heard.

It's a quarter to ten. I finally calm down, fold my arms under my head. I look at the ceiling and follow the shape made there by the bedside lamp. If your mother could see you—rummaging through people's stuff, it's the worst. Not really rummaging, I tell myself, feeling contrite now, yet unable to stop grinning: I didn't *touch* anything. God forbid he'd snoop around *my* closet, though! Assuming correctly that we would soon be moving into the bedroom, I had surreptitiously closed its sliding door beforehand, while he was still drinking coffee in the living room, night before last. The jumble, the mess: the record of a decade's worth of changing fashion, ever accumulating next to and alternating with what I happen to be wearing this year. A month ago, looking for a dress that subsequently proved to have been lost at a cleaner's, I came across a leftover miniskirt; appalled, I threw it out, then retrieved it and hung it back up; I'd had a good time in it, what a thrill it had been at first! And the beaten-down raincoat with the plaid lining, still from my sophomore year, and the slacks bought on sale at Bonwit's because they were made of such fine plaid wool, though they turned out not only to be too short that very fall, and the hem only half an inch deep, but nearly impossible to wear with what else I owned; yet I can't bring myself to get rid of them because they were a bargain and so very well made. The heaps, the junk, the odds and ends at the bottom of my closet—pointed-toe sling-back shoes that may do, in a pinch, under a long skirt; the ungainly rubber rain hat I wear once a year when it's pouring out and I need to get cigarettes; the Gucci bag that I haven't taken out of the closet for years now, but how thrilled I'd been when I'd bought it for nearly two weeks' worth of my salary, gleeful at having reached the heights of what I then considered New York elegance; belts that have fallen off their hooks, small red boots now long outgrown, left behind by the boy in the photograph on my mirror; the soccer jersey formerly belonging to a forgotten lover, which I wear while housecleaning...

So what did you learn from it all, I ask myself; what does it add up to besides your being a snoop? Well, he's neat, I tell myself. Plays tennis, skis, swims. Doesn't know the meaning of the word "laundromat." Are ten white, eight pink, and eleven blue shirts normal for a man of his age and profession? I have no idea. Though it's my age, too, I remind myself, more or less, and when do *I* ever own that many of anything? One thing I do know: I've never been with a man who has such a limited idea of the spectrum. Nothing purple, fuchsia, turquoise, orange—all right; but nothing brown? Nothing green, nothing yellow, nothing red? Those tiny maroon things on the ties don't count. Everything's blue or gray or white or black, except for those pink shirts, of course.

This is an unusual man you're getting mixed

up with, I tell myself. Never mind the clothes he's got, what about the clothes he hasn't got. I make a list, on a thick sheet of stationery. His pen gives my usually small, narrow-spaced handwriting a slant and breadth I'm not accustomed to. No bathrobe, I write—so what. One pair of pajamas kept under wraps? Maybe to have on hand in case he has to go to a hospital in a hurry, bought in the spirit in which mothers tell one not to rely on safety pins in underwear.... No scarf, no hat: probably immune to head colds. But why does this man not own any jeans? Do I know anyone—anyone—who doesn't have at least one pair, even if no longer worn, just one last pair left over from the sixties? And no turtlenecks. No leather jacket, no blazer, not a single, solitary, measly little T-shirt! Where are the corduroy pants I'm used to on men, where are the sandals, where are the sport jackets, the plaid flannel shirts?

I study my list. "It's O.K."; his cheerful voice in the other room raised now. "Never mind, I was glad to do it, glad we're done, too. See you tomorrow, relax, you've got nothing to worry about...." I swing my legs off the bed, sit up straight, fold the piece of paper along a sharp crease, stuff it into my handbag, which sits on the floor next to the bed. The front door slams, he's at the bedroom doorway, smiling: "Over, done, he's gone. Time to celebrate, sweetheart, you couldn't have been nicer about this mess, time to drink a little wine...."

Just before midnight we are lying on his bed. It turns out we drank no wine at all to begin with, but made love instead, hastily and with most of our clothes on; we've taken a shower together and I've told him it was my first in a decade, that I much prefer baths. Wrapped in towels, we ate three large pieces of blueberry pie left over from dinner and finished a bottle of Chablis. I am lying on my back, looking up at the ceiling, my arms under my head. He is stretched out on his stomach. His right arm supports his head while his left lies flat and lightly across my breasts. In the middle of the statistical tale he's requested from me— brothers and sisters and parents and grandparents, hometown, schools, jobs—I stop and close my eyes...please, I think, inarticulate even in my own mind, unable to turn to him and make the first move, please...He says into the silence, "I want to show you something." He leaves the room, returns with his shaving mirror, slaps my face, sits down on the edge of the bed. My head has fallen on one side onto the pillow. He takes a fistful of my hair and pulls me back until I look at him. He holds the mirror up for me to see and together we watch the symmetrical mark appear on my cheek. I stare at myself, mesmerized. I do not recognize this face; it is blank, a canvas there to display four smudges, red like war paint. He traces them gently.

Next day, during a business lunch with a client, I lose my train of thought in mid-sentence when last night's mirror image floats onto the surface of my brain. Desire sweeps over me so intense it makes me nauseous. I push away my plate and hide my hands under the napkin. I want to cry when I think it's another four hours before I see him.

So it went, a step at a time. And since we saw each other every night; since each increment of change was unspectacular in itself; since he made love very, very well; since I was soon crazy about him, not just physically, but especially so, it came about that I found myself—after the time span of a mere two weeks—in a setup that would be judged, by the people I know, as pathological.

It never occurred to me to call it pathological. I never called "it" anything. I told no one about it. That it was me who lived through this period seems, in retrospect, unthinkable. I dare only look back on those weeks as on an isolated phenomenon, now in the past; a segment of my life as unreal as a dream, lacking all implication.

"IT'S UNUSUAL FOR a man to have cats," I say. "Isn't it?" We are watching Cronkite: a dear, familiar face forever arranged—beneath an appropriate layer of surface concern—into the reassuring alignment of dependable benevolence... a faraway earthquake, the less faraway threat of yet another transit strike, Dow Jones up by two points. "Are you kidding?" he says wearily. "Don't I know it! Dogs, that's a different story. But not one man I know, who's not married that is, owns even one cat, let alone more." "Hm," I say. "Cats are for kids and little old ladies, if you ask me," he continues. "Or farms, or whatever." "Well," I say, "then why—" "They're nothing but a nuisance," he interrupts. "At least these don't shed much," I offer feebly; and finally I say, "Nobody's *forcing* you to keep cats."

"That's a laugh," he says. "That's a real laugh, if I do say so. You have absolutely no idea...."

There are three cats in his apartment, all equally homely. They are as oblivious of him as he seems of them. While he provides them with food and fresh water and a daily change of litter, he seems to take doing this for granted in much the same way in which they expect the regular presence of these commodities. There is no observable exchange of affection between them, or only if one chooses so to interpret a cat's slow progress across his prone body, and his wordless tolerance of such behavior; a questionable interpretation at best, considering the lack of expression these encounters evoke in either cat or man.

He is sitting on the couch. I'm sitting on two bed pillows on the floor, one of his calves at either side of me, my back against the couch, neck and shoulders supported by its front edge; my head, bent back, rests between his thighs. He plays with my hair: taking up strand after strand and curling each around a finger; pushing four fingers under a section of hair, lifting it up, and pulling it gently away from the skin; rubbing a small area of scalp at a time, his hands moving slowly across my head, over and over.

Cronkite bids us good-night and we watch the ensuing game show and then a program consisting entirely of policemen alternately involved in car chases and crashes. The repetitive images (at the end of the news he has turned off the sound) form a soothing and oddly appropriate accompaniment to the story of the cats, which he unfolds for me at leisure.

The first one came into his life along with the woman who lived with him briefly four years ago. She had just moved her cat into his apartment when she was offered a lucrative position in Zurich and decided to live abroad. The cat stayed behind—with him. For a number of months he continued to think of himself as only a stopgap caretaker of the animal, which appeared, from the first, to feel at home: mangy, scruffy, with a nearly bald tail and as eager an assortment of ambiguous colors as the garments that have been popular for the last several winters: fashioned from a substance enigmatically referred to as "fun fur," imitating the concept and construction, if not the appearance, of an early American quilt. He tried, at first energetically, to relocate the cat. But he was soon forced to acknowledge that the people he knew (some of whom would have taken in a kitten, while others might have been tempted by a Siamese) were hard put to disguise, for the duration of their awkward visits, how appalled they were at the thought of welcoming this particular animal into their attractive and carefully assembled Manhattan apartments. At one point he even placed an ad in the *Times*. Though he listed both his home and his office number, and though the ad ran five consecutive days, he received not one call in response. Off and on, as the months went by, he considered giving the cat to an animal shelter. But he decided to put off such a solution, at least for the time being. This sort of option, he thought, would always be open to him; in the meantime, something more suitable might turn up.

A year later he housed his eleven-year-old niece, in New York for a spelling contest in which she did not place. In gratitude for the care with which he had shown the girl around town, her mother—his sister—presented him with a second cat, apparently in a manner that made refusal impossible. "It was just a kitten, not much better looking than the old one, and out of its gourd for the first couple of days and the other one no help at all, snarling and carrying on as if I'd brought in a boa constrictor. After a while, somehow or other, they ended up getting along.

"Then one night I come home and I see some kids in the alley. They move off but, you know, making a big deal out of being casual. So I go back there like a fool and on the ground, what can I tell you, it was in pretty bad shape. I go upstairs like a sane man, and fix myself a drink and start reading the paper, thinking: in an hour it'll be gone. And an hour later I tell myself, *you need another cat like a hole in the head.*

"And I think, if anything, somebody should kill it, not pick it up, it's too far gone. I cook myself some eggs, I eat a salad, I have some coffee; I tell myself I'll go for a walk after the eleven o'clock news. Sure enough, it's still there, only somebody's pushed it over by the garbage cans. So I take a newspaper out of the trash and bring it up here and next morning I think, what am I, a nurse, and take it to the vet where I'd had the other two spayed, and by the time I picked it up, six days later, it was pretty chipper. Should've been, for $68.80. And every time I go out of town I have to have my cleaning lady come in all the way from Queens; and sometimes she can't, and not one of my friends has the sense to live around here and I can't very well ask somebody who won't take money for it to come all the way down from Central Park West in the Eighties, or from Sixty-fifth and York, or from godforsaken Brooklyn Heights. Even Andy, Thirtieth and Park to here isn't exactly a five-minute stroll. And the kid down the hall had to go away to Michigan State, *Michigan State*, Chrissakes! That leaves him out. So now I keep rotating a couple of other neighbors and I hate asking favors of people I'd just as soon never lay eyes on...."

"They don't shed much," I say, for the second time this evening, and he says, "big deal."

I WENT TO work every day, an articulate businesswoman, liked by my friends, valued by my superiors. At 5 P.M. sharp I cleared my desk, exchanged pleasantries with colleagues going down in the elevator, and went home—to his apartment. I went to mine only to pick up clothes and later, once a week, the mail. In the mornings we took the same subway line back to work, sharing the *Times:* a well-shaven man in a pin-striped business suit, carrying an attaché case—good teeth, charming smile; I with my own briefcase and my summer handbag and heels and lip gloss and freshly washed hair. An attractive, well-educated couple in New York City, average, middle-class, civilized.

"UP, UP, time to get up," he shouts from the doorway. He is holding a scuffed metal TV tray with a plate of scrambled eggs, three toasted English muffins, a pot of tea, one cup. A peeled, sectioned orange sits in a small wooden salad bowl. He grins broadly above the tray. "What on earth is this rush," I say. "It's nine-thirty, please..." I push both pillows behind me against the wall, sit up, smooth the blanket over my legs. "And it's Saturday!" He sets down the tray and mops up the few drops of spilled tea with the roll of paper towels he has brought along, clutched under his left arm. "It's Saturday," I repeat. "I hope you don't want to go anywhere, I don't want to see a soul. I want to stay right here and sleep until noon and the rest of the day I want to do nothing more strenuous than calling my sister and reading next week's *TV Guide*."

"Sounds exciting," he says. "You can do that when we get back. I have to go to Bloomingdale's." "You better go back to playing on those indoor courts," I say. "You've clearly been in the sun too long. No way will I go to Bloomingdale's on a Saturday." "It'll take no more than half an hour, I swear. An hour and a half, all in all. Half an hour up, half there, half an hour back. The sooner you stop talking and eat, the quicker we'll be done. You'll be back in bed by eleven-thirty."

We are halfway down the block when I say, "You're not by any chance walking toward the subway, are you?" He nods, blankly. "Absolutely not," I say. "I have to take that thing twice a day all week long, I'm not setting foot in it on a weekend." We get a cab at the corner. Bloomingdale's teems. "I always think these people are at the Hamptons this time of year," I say loudly. "Do they all come back every Saturday just to stock up?" "Half an hour, I promise you," he says. "All *right*," I say. "It's *you* who doesn't like stores, I like stores fine, I've got some sense about when I go in them, too." "Listen, sweetheart," he says, "will you please shut up, I'm asking you nicely. I'm being very patient under this petty cynicism, but pretty soon I'll tie you to the men's makeup counter and you'll end up buying a lot of Braggi bronzer and not having a good time at all until I come back." This vision makes me giggle. "What are you looking for?" I say. We're on the fifth floor. "A bed," he says. "A bed!" I exclaim. "You've got a perfectly good bed." "It's a great bed," he says. "So?" "It's a great bed for one person."

He is steering me past opulent dining room sets. There is one particularly dramatic group: small, piercing spotlights illuminate a black glass tabletop above obligatory chrome legs; black napkins are coiled inside black crystal rings, black glasses sit next to black bowls. "It's to serve caviar on charred steak," he stage-whispers to me, while we both almost stumble into a momentous arrangement of innumerable sofa sections, taking up more floor space than is offered by my entire apartment. "White velvet," I say. "Good God! One speck of cigarette ash, one cat hair, and poof it goes, all down the drain." "Bloomingdale customers are a clean lot," he says, gravely. "It may be a mystery to you, but it's very simple. We keep our pets in the john and smoke only in closets...." "...hear you're going on vacation Monday," says a woman's voice behind us. "Yup," answers a man's. "Where're you off to?" I look over my shoulder. A red-haired woman, elegantly dressed and holding a pad of sales slips, is speaking to a man in a Cardin suit, also holding such a pad. *"New York Ci-ty,"* he says, his mocking inflection of pride making them both laugh. "Smart man," she says, walking away, "best place in..." "Come *on*," I say—the massive sofas have been a fluke, we're amid more dining sets—"I'm not *that* big, and if you'd only said something, I'd have stayed on my side more."

"It's not the size," he says.

"Then what is it?" I persist. He stops before a fantasy room, a black-lacquered desk facing us at an angle. It supports, on its flawless and gleaming surface, one huge-bottomed lamp, six ceramic jars in assorted sizes, a narrow vase holding eight glorious tulips, a stack of oversized current photography books, a collection of artfully arranged foreign magazines, and an address book, covered in finely patterned silk. "Now this is what I like to see," he muses. "A real working desk. You can roll up your sleeves, spread out to your heart's content over all of two square inches, and get down to business." "Stop sneering," I say. "Nobody made you come here and that address book makes my mouth water. That's what all this stuff is supposed to do and it works." He smiles and puts his arm around me.

The bedrooms are next. The first one has a polished dark floor, the next is light parquet, a third is tiled in red; there is a bed with a headboard like a barndoor supporting the cloth-covered canopy, matching satiny fabric spilling to the floor on either side. A large plant inside a decorative and even larger basket sits inexplicably on the bedspread, slightly off-center. Another bed is staked out by four fat, spiral-turned posts. Six small pillows, covered in various but harmonizing prints, stand in orderly fashion on end against the bedpillows that presumably reside beneath the lush bulge in the spread. "*That's* what you need," I say. "I need a lot of little toy pillows?" "About four great big fat ones. Those two stingy flat ones of yours are a pain, you can't ever really lean against them comfortably." "What's to lean at, in bed," he says. "When you brought me breakfast this morning, just an example. Lots of times. It's great watching TV in bed or reading." "I don't actually do that," he says slowly, making me laugh. We pass a combination steel-brass bed, gray rods, big yellow bulbous things at the corners. An all-brass one is next: massive, impossibly curlicued at the same time, the most ornate bed I've ever seen. I stop before it. From a puffy quilt sewn in a pink and white starburst pattern embroidered eyelet cascades to the floor. A round table is covered like the bed, its skirt consisting of the same four frothy layers of flounces; at right angles to us reposes a majestic chaise longue, its white wood frame edged in gilt.

"Do you like this?" he asks. "Like a stage set," I say, "made to order for a heartbroken, sixteen-year-old Judy Garland." "Just the bed, I mean."

"It's nice enough in its garish way," I say. "The headboard and the footboard, they're like parts of a gate to some fairy-tale grounds, all that's needed is some brass birds mixed in with the rest of the swirls, and a monster head or two."

He motions to the red-haired woman who earlier wished the pale salesman a happy vacation. "When can I have this bed delivered?" I gasp. He squeezes my arm sharply. "This particular bed, sir"—she smiles firmly, first at him, then at me—"I would have to check, if you'll be seated for a moment, my desk is just over there." "You have gone out of your mind," I whisper. "A red face and a deranged brain, all from being outdoors a few times. . . ." He watches me; he does not smile. "Can you imagine what this baroque wonder is going to look like in your monk's gymnasium of a bedroom?" The saleswoman is off the phone. "There won't be any problem at all, sir, they're about to change the display. If you tell me where you want the bed delivered I can tell you into what delivery area you fall and on what days of the week our men are in that area."

"I'll need to check something," he says, once she has written down his address. The saleswoman and I follow him back to the stage set. It is closed off by a chain made of large plastic links. "May we go in?" he asks and then all three of us are standing at the foot of the bed. "It is one of our most—" He interrupts her: "I'm afraid my friend needs to lie down on this bed before I am able to make a decision." His voice is impeccably courteous. "I hope you don't mind." And to me: "Maybe you should take your shoes off." People always try on mattresses by lying down on them in public, in stores, I tell myself, but something makes blood rise into my neck and face. I take off my sandals, sit down on the bed, swing my legs up, and lower my back onto the star-quilted bedspread. "Lie in the middle," he says. I follow the glistening swirls above my feet with my eyes and move over carefully, supporting my weight as best I can on my hands and the heels of my feet, trying not to disturb the quilt. "Stretch your arms above your head and hold on to the headboard with your hands," he says. I think: it's a Saturday at Bloomingdale's, where's everybody gone to, this place is like a morgue; I could jump off the bed, leap over the chain, run to the escalator, go to a movie. ... "Come on, sweetheart," he says neutrally, "we don't have all day." The brass is icy in my hands. I close my eyes. "Spread your legs." "Your delivery area is Thursday." "Spread your legs." "You will be happy to hear that you will have this bed next Thursday." "Spread your legs." "Our delivery men are in your area Thursdays and Fridays, but I will personally ascertain that your delivery date will be Thursday." I do as he says.

I buckle my sandals, avoiding the eyes of a couple holding hands beyond the plastic chain. "Do you have mattresses?" She clears her throat, her voice smooth again. "Bedding is on four, but I can sell you a mattress and box spring from that floor, too." "Will you pick a hard mattress and box springs and have everything shipped at the same time?" "But, sir, you will want to select..." "I won't," he says. "A Posturepedic maybe..." "Fine," he says. "But what about the type of ticking..." "It would please me very much if you'd pick the kind you like best," he says and smiles at her, a tall man in tennis shoes and old khaki pants, a white tennis shirt, his nose peeling, skin more red than tan on his arms and throat and face. "Yes, of course," she says, smiling up at him in return. "And four fat pillows," he says. "Goose down or Dacron? I'll need to know their sizes...." "Just pillows," he says. Neither of us speaks on the way home.

When I stop by my apartment a few days later, I find a box from Bloomingdale's containing a silk-covered address book.

WE'RE DOING ERRANDS: supermarket, liquor store, dry cleaner's, drugstore. It's a lovely Saturday, a week after our trip to Bloomingdale's (the bed arrived on Thursday as promised), in early June. We spend a long time at the toothpaste counter: he is giving dramatic recitals of competing TV commercials—BETTER CHECKUPS wins. I think: I've never been this much in love before. Twice I ask out loud, "How can I be so happy?" Each time he smiles at me, a delighted grin, and shifts both shopping bags onto one arm to hug my shoulders with the other.

We are both laden down with packages when he says, "I have to get one more thing," and hails a cab. We end up in Brooklyn, at a small, obscure hunting store. There are two clerks, one dignified and elderly, one in his teens, no other customers. He is pricing insulated vests, the kind to be worn under windbreakers.

I put my parcels on a chair, walk around, get bored, sit down on the edge of an old mahogany desk, pick up and leaf through a three-year-old *New Yorker*, which miraculously looks brand-new. "This one, I guess," he says. I look over at the counter, he is looking back at me. He is holding a riding crop: "I'd like to try it out." There is a peculiar shift: from one second to the next I have become disoriented, I am on alien territory, in a foreign century. He walks a few steps to where I am half-sitting on the desk, one foot on the floor, the other dangling. He pulls my skirt up over my left leg, which is resting on the desk, steps back, and strikes me across the inner thigh. The searing pain is an inextricable part of a wave of excitement that robs me of breath and speech and the ability to move; every cell in my body is awash with lust. It is silent in the small, dusty room. The clerks behind the counter have frozen. He slowly smooths down my skirt and turns to the older man, who is wearing a suit and still looks like an accountant, though a deep flush is spreading upward from his shirt collar. "This one will do."

WHAT HE DID

*He fed me. He bought all food, cooked all meals, washed all dishes.

*He dressed me in the morning, undressed me at night, and took my laundry to the cleaner's along with his. One evening, while taking off my shoes, he decided they needed resoling and took them to the shoemaker the next day.

*He read to me endlessly: newspapers, magazines, murder mysteries, Katherine Mansfield short stories, and my own files when I brought them home to catch up on work.

*Every three days he washed my hair. He dried it with my hand dryer and was clumsy at it only the first two times. One day he bought an outrageously expensive Kent of London hairbrush and beat me with it that evening. Its bruises persisted beyond all others. But every night he used it to brush my hair. Neither before nor since has my hair been brushed so thoroughly, for such long periods at a time, so lovingly. It shone.

*He bought tampons for me and inserted and extricated them. When I was dumbfounded the first time he said, "I eat you while you're menstruating and we both like that. There's no difference."

*He ran my bath every night, experimenting with different gels, crystals, and oils, taking an adolescent girl's delight in buying great varieties of bath products for me, while sticking steadfastly to a routine of showers, Ivory soap, and Prell Concentrate for himself. I never stopped to contemplate what his cleaning woman thought of the whip lying on the kitchen counter, of the handcuffs dangling from the dining room doorknob, of the snakes' heap of narrow, silvery chains coiled in the corner of the bedroom. I did idly wonder what she thought of this sudden proliferation of jars and bottles, nine barely used shampoos crowding the medicine chest, eleven different bath salts lined up on the edge of the tub.

*Every night he took my makeup off. If I live to be a hundred, I won't forget how it felt to sit in an armchair, my eyes closed, my head thrown back, while the gentle pressure of a cotton ball soaked in lotion moved across my forehead, over my cheeks, lingered at length on my eyelids. . . .

WHAT I DID

*Nothing.

He comes home annoyed. One of his tennis partners has told him that Tender Vittles is junk, rotting cats as eating nothing but Rice Crispies and marshmallows would rot a human. " 'Glossy coats,' he says to me, Andy the expert, not a cat to his name, all he knows comes from the woman he's been breaking up with for five years now, and she once owned a Burmese. I can see how you'd tell if a black cat suddenly starts running around without a shine, but these? They get bigger, they get fatter, they're less of a wreck, but their *coats*, for Christ's sake, they just look like what they've always looked like. 'Do your cats have glossy coats?' he says to me. How the hell should *I* know?"

That night he empties three cans of Chicken of the Sea tuna into the cats' bowls. Next morning, dressed for work, he prepares and sets out three combinations made of five beaten eggs: one third poured over a fresh heap of

---

tuna, one by itself in a bowl, a third part stirred into milk in yet another bowl. At 6:30 P.M., walking straight into the kitchen, he unwraps a pound of chopped beef and crumbles it onto a dinner plate. He owns few dishes and has run out of bowls.

The cats have gone on a fast. Not one of them has so much as tried a mouthful of the new fare. None has deigned to sniff at the various dishes obstructing the kitchen floor, or not, at any rate, beyond the cursory attention even an empty cigarette pack commands from them. At 9 P.M. he goes back to the kitchen. I follow him. He points at the arrangement of three cat bowls, three salad bowls, and one white china plate with a worn gold rim around a border of pink and mauve sprigs of flowers— a castoff formerly belonging to the aunt who has given him the heavy damask tablecloth he keeps forever on his dining room table, the cloth that reminds me of some Salvation Army special. "You see?" he asks. "By now they'd have eaten this stuff if it were good for them. If only they can lay their hands on it, animals eat what their bodies need, they're not like people, that's what the fat guy at the market told me." And tearing open one Liver-, one Seafood-, and one Chicken-flavored envelope of Tender Vittles—three cats purring in unison at the sound—he says under his breath, "That's right, gang, the health food fad's over."

I AM STANDING, nearly on tiptoes, across the room from him, my arms raised above my head. My hands are tied to the hook on the wall on which his one large painting hangs during the day. My end of the room is dark, only the reading lamp over his shoulder is lit. He has told me to be quiet. The TV is on, but he is making notes on a legal pad, absorbed in his work, and doesn't look up for what seem to me long periods of time. My arms begin to ache and then my entire body and finally I say, "Listen, I can't stand it, really...."

He gives me a quizzical look and goes into the bedroom, comes back with two handkerchiefs, and says in a polite, conversational tone of voice, "I want you to shut the fuck up." He stuffs most of one handkerchief into my mouth and ties the second one tightly across it. I taste the bland flavor of sizing.

Sixty Minutes begins. I try to listen, stare at the back of the set, attempting to visualize each commercial in order to distract myself from the waves of pain rolling over me. I tell myself that surely my body must soon go numb but my body does nothing of the sort, it just hurts. Then it hurts even more and, by the time *Sixty Minutes* is over, muffled sounds come through the handkerchief, which is lodged way back in my throat and holds my tongue down flat. He gets up and walks over toward me and turns on the floor lamp next to his desk, adjusting the shade so the light shines into my eyes. For the first time since I've known him I begin to cry. He looks at me inquisitively, leaves the room, and comes back holding the bottle of bath oil he has bought me on the way home from work. He begins to rub oil into my neck and armpits. Everything in my brain is blocked out by the convulsive spasms in my muscles. He massages my breasts and I'm fighting for air through my nose, which is flooded with tears. Now there is oil on my stomach, a slow, insistent, rhythmic, circular motion. I'm suddenly in terror, convinced I'm choking, I am really going to choke, in another minute I'll be dead, when he spreads my legs, which stretches me even more. I scream. It is a muted sound, like a child's pretend foghorn, totally ineffectual from behind all that cloth. For the first time tonight he looks interested, fascinated even. His eyes are three inches from mine and something is moving very lightly up and down alongside my clitoris. His fingers are slippery with oil, drenched in oil, and in mid-scream my body shifts gear to the sounds—not so dissimilar—that it makes when I'm about to come and then I come.

He unties me, fucks me standing up, puts me to bed, bathes my face with a washcloth dipped in cold water from a white Tupperware bowl. He rubs my wrists for a long time. Just before I fall asleep he says, "You'll have to wear long sleeves tomorrow, sweetheart, what a nuisance, it's going to be a hot day."

OUR EVENINGS RARELY VARIED. He ran my bath, undressed me, handcuffed my wrists. I soaked in the tub while he changed his clothes and started dinner. When I was ready to get out I called him. He pulled me up, slowly soaped my body, rinsed and dried me off. Unclasped the handcuffs, put one of his shirts on me—white or pink or pale blue broadcloth, shirts made to be worn with a suit, the sleeves covering my fingertips, a fresh shirt every night, crisp from the Chinese laundry—put the handcuffs back on. I watched him prepare dinner. He was an excellent though limited cook, going through the four or five dishes he did well, then fixing omelettes or a steak for a couple of nights, then starting all over again. He always drank wine while washing the salad greens and would give me a sip from his glass whenever he took one himself. He talked about what had happened at his office, I told him about what had happened at mine. The cats took turns rubbing against my bare legs.

When dinner was ready he put one very large serving on one plate. We went to the dining room—barely enough space to walk comfortably around the table and three chairs on a worn, deep red oriental carpet—by far the most colorful of his three rooms; where the rug left off, the bright and intricately patterned fabric made up of backs of books took over, flowing from floor to ceiling on two walls, leaving space only for a window and door on the other two. He kept the table covered with that treasured damask tablecloth. I sat at his feet, tied to the table leg. He took a mouthful of fettucine, then fed one to me; stabbed at a forkful of Boston lettuce, guided the next one to my mouth, wiped the salad oil off my lips and his in turn. A sip of wine, then the lowered glass for me to drink from. Sometimes he tilted it too sharply so that the wine spilled over my lips and slid down the sides of my face onto my neck and chest. He would kneel before me and suck the wine off my nipples.

Often, during dinner, he pushed my head between his thighs. We developed a game: he tried to see how long he could continue to eat calmly; I, how soon I could make him drop his fork and moan. When I once told him that I was becoming particularly fond of the taste of him followed by vegetable curry, he laughed and laughed and said, "Jesus, I'm going to make enough tomorrow to last us all week."

When we were finished he would go to the kitchen to wash the dishes and make coffee—abominable coffee, it never varied—which he carried into the living room on a tray: one pot of coffee, one cup, one saucer, one brandy glass. (After we'd known each other for a month, confirmed coffee addict though I am, I finally switched to tea.) Then he read to me, or we both read our separate books. My looking up was the signal for him to turn my page. Or we watched TV, or we worked. Above all we talked, literally for hours. I had never talked this much with anyone. He learned my life history, in minute detail; I became equally familiar with his. I would have recognized his college friends on sight, known from his boss's position in his chair what mood he was in. I adored his jokes and his very manner of telling them, in a slow, bored voice, a fiercely deadpan expression. His favorites were stories about my grandfather, my favorites were his tales about his three years in India. . . .

We never went out, saw friends only at noon. A few times he begged off invitations by phone, rolling his eyes at me while gravely explaining how swamped he was with work, while I giggled. Throughout most evenings I was tied to the couch or the coffee table, within touching distance of him.

IT'S WEDNESDAY, we've known each other three weeks, and we're meeting for lunch. It is the one lunch we'll eat together on a working day, though our offices are only a $1.05 cab ride apart. It is a midtown restaurant: as noisy as the streets outside, fluorescent lights, a scowling crowd waiting at the door to be seated. We sit across from each other in the glare, he orders roast beef sandwiches and wine.

I've had a minor triumph in the morning, a project I've been pushing for months has come through. I go on about it happily: "It's not such a big deal in itself but it's exciting to me because all along it looked as if . . ." He puts his thumb diagonally across my lips. His fingers cup my left cheek. "I want to hear all about it. There'll be lots of time tonight. Leave your mouth open."

He takes his hand from my face and dips his thumb into my glass of wine; the liquid, a deep red in the glass, turns pink and transparent on his skin. He wets my lips with it. His thumb moves slowly, my mouth is slack under his touch. Then across my upper teeth, from left to right, back along the lower teeth from right to left. Finally his thumb comes to rest on my tongue. I think, without alarm, idly: we're in broad daylight. . . .

A slight pressure on my tongue prompts me to begin to suck his thumb. It tastes salty under the wine. When I stop he pushes gently and I resume and only when my stomach melts do I close my eyes.

He is smiling when he retrieves his thumb. He holds his palm above my plate and says, "Dry me off." I wrap his hand in my napkin as if stilling blood. Instead of the untouched sandwich before me I see myself, tied to the bed, tied to the dining room table, tied to the legs of the bathroom sink, flushed amid the steam while he takes a shower; I listen to the water roar, sweat beads itching on my upper lip, my eyes closed, my mouth open; tied and stripped, tied and reduced to a single frenzy: craving more.

"Don't forget," he says. "Sometimes during the day I want you to remember how it is with you . . ." and then, "Drink your coffee." I sip the lukewarm fluid decorously, as if by permission. He stirs me out of the restaurant. Two hours later I give up and call him. The spell has remained unbroken. I have stared at my calendar, I have stared out of my window at the grid of windows across the street. I have not taken my calls. His secretary warns me crisply that he has an appointment in five minutes, then there's his voice. "You can't do this to me," I whisper into the phone. There is a short silence. "I'm cooking shrimp tonight," he says slowly, "think about that."

THE LUNCH WAS a turning point. It made clear—to both of us—that my life was split, neatly, in two: day and night; with him/without him. And that it was a mistake and possibly dangerous to mix the two. Day by day, week by week, the two segments of my life edged into an increasingly complete balance. The clearer, the more focused, the more "fantastic" our evenings became, the more did my working life slip into fantasy.

It was a pleasant enough fantasy. I did well within it, better, in fact, than I had while my office, my clients, my work, had been serious matter, hard-core reality. As is only right in one's fantasy, I was at ease, relaxed, calm. I won a new account one day, charmed a colleague into peace after months of altercations the next. I worked tirelessly, suspended. Minor annoyances over which I would have fretted in the past—a phone call not returned, a longer than reasonable wait for a client's decision, a coffee stain on my sleeve half an hour into my day—no longer mattered.

The reality of my days was replaced by surface equanimity and a blandness to the core. My lunches bland, going past me unnoticed, mingling bland and friendly talk with bland and friendly people—friends, clients, colleagues, all the same. I moved through the subways, noting the fortuitous combination of light and dark blues on the ceiling posts. Above ground, cabs a pleasant yellow, once I counted nine taxis in a row down Park Avenue. A dream city without debris seen by someone drugged, or by a severely nearsighted woman bravely and foolishly at large without glasses. Crowds that automatically and amiably part to let me through. Every day a different movie, none burdened by a plot, or only toying with a plot so languid as to reveal no connections, no power to engage me beyond its agreeable surface; always only hours away from reality, taking time-out from what counted, what really went on in my life; a breathing spell from the exhilarating and inexorable plot unfolding at night.

The nights were palpable and fierce, razors, outlined so clearly as to be luminous. A different country, its landscape and currency plain: heat, fear, cold, pleasure, hunger, glut, pain, desire, overwhelming lust.

There was sharp pepper that made me gasp, and the shock of chili burning my throat, and Chablis like gold smoothing my vocal cords, a simple chocolate pudding he'd made from a Royal mix invading my blood. My body alive and pliant around me, soon to turn liquid or afire, either way. Every night, looking down at myself after a bath—flecks of foam on my nipples and pubic hair, one palm docile inside the other, wrists accustomed to lying against one another, glinting steel as natural as silver combs in one's hair and as decorative—every night now, I reveled in my beauty.

Years ago, once the frenzied adolescent obsession had calmed itself, I had sized up my body and decided that it was all right. I knew very well which parts of me would look better were they shaped differently, but had not worried over such acknowledged deficiencies for over a decade. Whenever I did fall into the trap of criticizing too harshly, I told myself that for every demonstrable inequity there was something pleasing to point to, resulting, all together, in an acceptable balance. But now, under his eyes and hands...

I had neither jumped rope nor jogged in the park, I had not lost or gained a pound, it had to be, after all, the same body in which I had lived since adulthood. But there it was, unrecognizable, transformed: supple, graceful, polished, adored. The flesh leading to the crook of an elbow, where two cerulean veins fade into opaque skin, exquisitely soft; a belly like silk sloping gently toward hipbones; an upper arm joining my torso to form a delicate fold like that at the center of a young girl's pubic mound; a shallow, oval hollow at the inside of a thigh, leading upward from the knee, smoothing gently, giving way to a slow ripening, downy white infinitely sensitive, the finest fabric in the world . . .

"I HAVE TO go to a meeting," he says. "It's the wrap-up of the Handlemayer thing, just a formality, it shouldn't take long." He is getting dressed again, having finished the dinner dishes: a different suit, though identical in cut to the one he took off two hours ago, dark gray now instead of dark blue. A fresh, light blue shirt, twin to the one I'm wearing, a dark gray silk tie with small, wine-red dots arranged into diamond shapes. He says, "I'd like you to do something before I leave."

He leads me into the bedroom and says, "Lie down." He ties my ankles to the footboard, my left wrist to the headboard. He sits down on the bed beside me. He slides his right hand up my right thigh, polishes my hipbone under his palm, brushes the skin on my stomach with that part of the hand with which TV Orientals deal karate chops. He rests his thumb on my navel for a moment, exerting the gentlest of pressure, then opens the two fastened buttons of my shirt and, with both hands, slowly pushes the fabric aside. The sleeves of his suit jacket brush my nipples.

My breathing has been irregular since he first told me to lie down; whenever he touches me I hold my breath, then breathe rapidly and shallowly until his next touch. I cannot keep my head still on the pillow. He takes my free right hand. Holding my palm, looking at me all the while, he sucks each of my fingers until they drip with saliva. He guides my hand between my legs and says, "I'd like to watch you make yourself come."

He is sitting idly, comfortably, one leg crossed over the other, the creases sharp in the freshly cleaned suit. I do not try to move my hand. He waits. "You don't understand." My voice cracks. "I never..." He is silent. "I've never done that in front of anybody. It embarrasses me."

He picks up the package of Winstons from the bedside table, puts a cigarette in his mouth, lights it, draws on it ineptly, eyes squinted, puts it between my lips. A moment later I need to move my hand to hold the cigarette. "It embarrasses her," he repeats. His tone of voice is bland, there is no mocking inflection, nor is there a trace of anger in what he says next. "You're pretty dense, aren't you? You haven't caught on yet what we're all about."

Without disturbing the cigarette, he takes my watch from my free wrist. "I'll be back in a couple of hours, no later." He turns off the bedside lamp, then the lamp in the corner, and closes the bedroom door quietly.

I am shaken and, at the moment, concerned more than anything that I should be able to light another cigarette after this one. There is the saucer I use for an ashtray on the bedside table and the pack of Winstons, but he has put the lighter he bought for himself—to light my cigarettes—back into his pocket. There are no matches in sight. I put the half-smoked cigarette into one corner of my mouth, retrieve the pack, shake one cigarette loose, put the pack on my stomach, move the ashtray next to my right hip. Then an awkward turning and reaching and stretching, but I manage it, though crushing the pack as I roll over: I transfer the half-smoked cigarette to the hand bound to the headboard, hold the fresh cigarette to the lit one with my free hand, wait, put it into my mouth. The third time it lights. I do not ask myself why I'm not thinking clearly enough to simply put an unlit cigarette in my mouth and hold the lit one against it; nor do I ask myself why I refrain from untying myself, something I could accomplish more easily and surely more quickly than the sweaty fumbling I've just been through. . . .

My face burns again at the thought of him—anyone—watching me. I think: this is the first time I've said no. Then: that's nonsense, melodrama. I've explained something to him, that's all, something he doesn't know about me. "He knows I'll do anything," I say out loud, though tentatively, into the faint whir of the air conditioner, at the shadows on the ceiling, to the shape that is his tall chest of drawers. I am appalled that it was me who said the words that now ring in my ears. I try to count what I wouldn't do. I once had anal intercourse with someone and it hurt and we stopped—but I would surely try it again, with him, should he want to. I've read how people urinate on each other, shit. I've never done that and the thought of it nearly makes me ill—surely he'd never want to do that, either. But how did I feel about being tied up and beaten, only weeks ago? And why should there be any difference between the various ways in which he makes me come and masturbating in front of him, if it pleases him? Yet the shame of it squints my eyes shut, turns my legs cold, grinds my teeth.

Nearly a decade ago, a good friend of mine had described to me how she and her lover masturbated together and how much she liked it. "Don't worry," she had said to me when I blurted out—not haltingly that time but with spontaneous horror—that I could never do that, would not, ever. "It's just your particular hang-up. We've all got them. I can't stand it when a man puts his tongue in my ear, gives me the creeps." She had laughed uproariously.

I say it out loud: "Hang-up. My hang-up." All at once I respect the word. No longer a flabby, anonymous catchall, a dark specter suddenly, precise: gallows in marketplaces, lynchings at noon, and then there he is at the door.

He turns on the bedside lamp, slips my watch back onto my wrist, carefully pushes the thin strap through both loops; I'm too impatient to do that and always stop after the first loop is secured, so that the second one is stiff from disuse. He says, "You started masturbating early." I laugh. "That's either a hunch or an accusation," I say. "How was the meeting?" He says nothing. I focus on the brass handles of the chest of drawers, fixing them sharply in my mind. "I guess, six, I don't remember." He prompts, "And often, as an adult." I begin one of the sentences I have rehearsed in his absence, reasonable sentences, adult sentences: choice and preference and the delicate balance of intimacy versus... I falter, leave the brass handles behind, face the window now, the need to turn away from him overpowering. He takes my face into both hands and draws it slowly back to the side of the bed where he is sitting. He speaks deliberately. "I want you with me, but I won't force you to stay." The air conditioner shifts gears, purrs. I open my mouth, he puts a finger gently across my lips. "This is how it is with us, listen. While you're with me, you do as I say. While you're with me," merely repeated, without added gravity, "you do as I say." And a moment later, disgruntled: "For Christ's sake, what's the big deal?" And finally, casually: "You could give it another try. You might want me to get you some cream. I could lower the lights." "It's the only thing," I say, my face turned back toward the window. "Ask me, I'll do anything else."

He picks up the bedside phone, dials a number from memory, gives his name, his address and mine, and says, "Fifteen minutes." He takes the largest of his suitcases from the top shelf of the closet, lays it open on the bedroom floor. I have brought those belongings of mine that are now scattered throughout his apartment in separate installments: a large straw basket once, a canvas overnight case another time, sometimes just things stuffed into a shopping bag. He takes my clothes, all on the left side of the closet, off the rod, folds them in half—still on his wooden suit hangers—and they lie neatly on the bottom of the suitcase. A scarf here, another one, the fountain pen he bought for me, so that I would stop using his, some books in the living room, half a dozen records, four pair of shoes, underwear jumbled in his second bureau drawer, the unopened bottle of Miss Dior he bought me last Saturday, and a second one, almost empty.

A trip to the kitchen. He returns with a large plastic garbage bag, I hear the bathroom paraphernalia clatter into the bag, he is back in the bedroom, the plastic bag takes up most of the suitcase. My hair dryer, my diary, the suitcase snaps shut. It has not taken him five minutes.

He unties me and rubs each ankle and my left wrist at length, though they were fastened loosely enough to show no marks. He gently tugs his blue shirt off my back. He has left out a summer sweater of mine, folded on a chair. I raise my arms automatically and he slips the pale wool over my head. And a gray linen skirt. I'm so used to being dressed by him that I wait for him to kneel before me on one knee while I step into the waistband. I think: I've never told him that I always put skirts on over my head; he thinks of skirts as the equivalents of pants, so naturally one steps into them, pulls them up. And: he's forgotten underwear, I surely can't be on the street at midnight with a skirt on and no underpants. Stepping into the open waist, watching him get up while he eases the skirt up over my hips; the lifting of the sweater while he pulls the zipper at my left side and fastens the hook and eye, the smoothing of thin wool over raw linen.

He holds up my sandals now and motions for me to sit on the bed. I hold out each foot in turn, flex the arch, watch him slip on the sandal and fasten the buckle. He stands behind me and brushes my hair. "I'll take you down to the taxi. If I find other things of yours, I'll drop them off."

His brush in my hair, the slow seductive strokes, the faint crackling of electricity. I turn and clutch his thighs. He holds very still. I am crying loudly as a child. Both of his hands are in my hair, the brush has fallen on the carpet.

"The cab'll be here any minute," he says, and the doorman's ring at that very moment. My voice, raised, "You can't," his bland at the intercom, "...kind enough to tell him I'll be right down," and to me, "I thought you had decided." And then the kneeling before him, not to satisfy him with my mouth as so often before but in abjection, the pleading incoherent yet clear: "Anything," and "Please." And his voice at the brass box again, smooth: "Give him five dollars, Ray, and tell him to wait, thank you very much." And his few steps back down the hall and into the bedroom and a thug's growl: "All *right*, then, *now*, *do* it." My

---

body pushed prone and the hem of my skirt scratchy around my neck. He takes his father's ring off his right hand, throws it on the bed above, holds me by the throat with the left hand, uses the ring-free right to slap my face, palm on left cheek, the back of his hand on the right, the palm again, "All *right*, then, let's see her *do* it." My own hand shoved into my mouth, "Make it *easy* for her, good and *wet*," and in the softest voice, a murmur, "I'll get you started, sweetheart, it'll be so simple." My thighs spread apart, heat springing up under his tongue and only a slight shift when he lifts his head and brings my hand to where he has begun what I am far too familiar with to try or want to fight, my fore and middle finger slipping down as always, and coming.

"I loved this," he says. "I love watching your face. You look so extraordinary when you come, you stop being pretty and turn into this thing, ravenous, with a stretched open mouth." And in the hallway, "Give him another five, Ray, tell him to go home."

NOTHING HAD PREPARED ME. Some years back I had read *The Story of O*, intrigued by the beginning, horrified after a few pages, repulsed long before the end. Sadomasochists in real life were black-leather freaks, amusing and silly in their ridiculous getups. If a friend, a peer, had told me she had herself tied to a table leg at home after a full day's work at the office—well, it has never come up. God knows I would not have believed it.

AT FOUR-THIRTY ON a Friday afternoon he calls me at work: "You'll be in room 312 at the Algonquin, at five-thirty." I've had lunch there once. A few days earlier, during yet another one of our interminable talks ("Let's compare restaurants"—"and hotels"—"there's the Paris Ritz"—"ridiculous"—"ZumZum, then"—"good bratwurst"—"lousy sauerkraut"—"mediocre coffee..."), I had told him how romantic the lobby had seemed to me, and the plush red corner where I had sat with two clients. They had long been inured to Algonquin charm and I told him how I had to suppress my enjoyment sufficiently to be able to concentrate on what they were saying.

I intend to go by subway but an elderly couple climbs out of a Checker in front of my office building just as I walk through the revolving glass. I hold the car door for them, listen to my thigh muscles ache as I repeat to myself, "You'll be... at five-thirty" and walk through the Algonquin doors minutes later. I knock at 312, twice, but there is no answer and the door is unlocked. I have assumed he would be waiting for me. I say his name at the bathroom door, which stands ajar, even—on an impulse only half-playful—open the closet. There is no one there.

The bed is piled high with packages. Not gift-wrapped, but what one spills on a bed after a day of shopping, just before Christmas. The room key is in the ashtray on the bedside table, his handwriting on a note stuck above the dial numbers on the phone. "Open them," it reads, "and take a bath and get dressed."

I start with one of the smaller shopping bags from Brooks Brothers. It contains a light blue shirt, like the ones I have been wearing at night, but smaller. Men's socks in an Altman's bag. A container that looks like a child's hat box holds a sandy beard and mustache wrapped in tissue paper. My hands shake a little by the time I unwrap the largest package: a dark gray suit and vest. Shoes next. A tie. A blond man's wig. A small packet of hairpins from Woolworth's. A white handkerchief. A man's summer hat.

I push the wrappings aside and sit down on the edge of the bed, holding the wig in both hands. It's an expensive wig, the hair human and soft to the touch. Alarm and excitement race inside me, side by side, like speeding cars on a dark highway. Every few moments they narrow the space between them and touch without noise or sparks, gently. Once I'm in the bathwater—Estée Lauder, Jean Naté, and Vitabath to choose from (but I can't, put careless amounts of each under the gushing faucets; they cancel each other out, for the first time in weeks I'm submerged in milky water without foam amid a confused mingling of scents)—alarm chooses a turnoff. Excitement hurtles me onward, dark miles stretching ahead, headlights illuminating only a few yards of gray road as I turn the virgin square of soap over and over between my palms.

I dry myself in the sequence in which he dries me every evening: face and neck, feet and calves, back and buttocks. The only thing missing from the costume now spread out on the bed is underwear. The trousers' lining is smooth against my skin. The socks fit, the shirt fits. My breasts are small enough so that the layers of shirt and vest and finally suit coat obscure them completely.

I put on the shoes—an old-fashioned wing-tip style, like his, the gleaming leather lining pungent, why don't women's shoes ever smell this delicious?—the left one feels tight at first.

There is a small pot of theatrical glue, a brush attached to the inside of the cap. I'm in a quandary, can't decide whether the glue goes

on the backing of the mustache and the beard
or on my skin. I end up spreading it thinly on
the backing, something like canvas, and
position the mustache under my nose. It tickles
and looks straight out of a high school play and
makes me laugh out loud. I need to make three
adjustments to get it to sit evenly above my
upper lip. The beard is harder. Again and
again, while the glue is setting and turning
sticky, I take it off and start over, repositioning
it, until it ends up at the same distance from my
earlobes on each side and stays put under my
chin. The wig, by comparison, is easy: I brush
my own hair into a scrawny ponytail high up on
my head, twist it, pin loose strands close to my
scalp all round. Once the wig is pulled over my
hair onto my head it fits tightly. I carefully lift
an upper layer of hair and anchor another few
pins through the canvas backing to my own
hair beneath. The wig's hair at the back of my
neck touches my shirt collar, almost covers my
ears at the sides, falls onto my forehead in a
thick wave.

In the process of replacing the tissue paper in
which the mustache has been wrapped, I find,
in the same round box, a set of eyebrows. I glue
them over my own. I have been scrutinizing
myself in the mirror above the dressing table all
along, but fixed on details. Now the mecha-
nism comes into play that allows one to switch

from focusing on a panel of glass, every dust particle and thumbprint important and distinct, to seeing the outside beyond, the windowpane gone. There is a face in the mirror, no longer an isolated beard or the tilt of a wig. Alarm screeches at me from an obscure sidestreet and collides with excitement before both continue to speed on side by side. I see that he looks ill at ease in a manner familiar to me, but I recognize nothing else. Across from me sits a slender, pleasant-looking young man. Were someone to introduce him to me at a party I'd register the involuntary response, a nod somewhere in me: possible. . . . He has wide gray eyes, thick blond hair, light bushy eyebrows, a fine nose; pale skin, a short, reddish-blond beard. Acknowledging the spark of a preliminary understanding between us, he leans toward me; he, too, likes what he sees. It lasts for only a moment. There is a violent wrenching inside me, alarm takes me over. The room swims, I cower on the floor at the foot of the bed, one sentence pounding in my chest: I want my mother.

That, too, passes. I push back the hair over my forehead, open the pack of Camels that is lying on the bedside table. I've never smoked a Camel and begin to cough immediately, my throat raw. But I inhale more deeply the second time and, perversely, the rough flavor clears my head, I'm no longer dizzy but clear-eyed and calm. I wonder, briefly, where to put the handkerchief. I can't remember where he keeps his and finally put it into the back trousers pocket. I have never worn a garment with back pockets before and slide my hand in and out of it, feeling the slippery lining and the curve of buttock beneath.

Only two items are left, the tie and the hat, and both give me trouble. The tie, I discover, comes with instructions: tucked into the tissue paper that is folded around the silk is a thin sheet of paper. He has done five diagrams. The heading reads: "What's on the drawing is what's in the mirror, follow step by step." The first time around the knot ends up an inch below the top collar button, the second time I get it right. The hat, however, is beyond me. I set it on top of my head carefully, then pull it down slightly, tilt it this way and that. I know enough about hats to realize it is my size, or, rather, the correct size for my own head and pinned-up hair and the wig, but no matter how I push at it, it looks odd. Not even trying to summon the hat angles of various male movie actors, or the appearance of my lone male friend who wears hats regularly, makes sense when applied to the image in the mirror.

I finally give up, reluctantly, and put the hat back in its box. It is seven o'clock on my wristwatch, which I take off and put into my handbag. I wash my hands. I stand in front of the full-length mirror, buttoning and unbuttoning the jacket, posing first with one, then the other hand in my pants pockets. Then, idly and smiling, I take off my earrings and put those, too, with the watch. And I discover the belt, while carefully folding the many wrappings, returning—as if following a specific assignment—each smoothed sheet of tissue into its appropriate box or bag.

The belt is identical to his, but stiffer. It fits into the palm of my left hand and slowly uncoils when I lay it on the bedspread. I run its length through thumb and forefinger, then close my hand into a fist around the buckle. I open it, wind the leather a few times across my palm and over the back of my hand, then close my fist once more. I am overwhelmed by the memory of a woman, her wrists tied to a shower head, writhing under the blows of this belt, which cuts through the curtain of water again and again. The phone rings. "I'm in the lobby," he says. "Come on down. Don't forget the room key."

I slip the key into my right jacket pocket, transfer it to the right pants pocket, put it into the left jacket pocket, anxiously now. I thread the belt through the trouser loops, fumble the buckle shut. I pick up the Camels and a book of matches, don't know where to put them, and end up holding them in my left hand. A balding, short man waits with me at the elevator for a moment, then mumbles under his breath and walks rapidly down the corridor. I look after him and realize that he is no shorter than I am. Wearing sandals with three-inch heels I am tall for a woman; now I'm a man of below average height.

A middle-aged woman stands at the back of the elevator. I step in and stand near the door. When we come to the first floor and I am about to walk out into the lobby, I remember. I step aside and she passes through the door on ahead, without looking at me. I am blushing and have to force myself not to smile. What an astonishing ritual, I think, and simultaneously, gleefully: I passed!

He is sitting on a corner sofa, motions me to the chair facing him across a low round table with a brass bell, his glass of scotch, an empty ashtray. He is wearing his gray suit, identical to mine. He looks at me for a long time, taking in the shoes, the fit of the vest, the knot of the tie, the beard and hair. "What about the hat?" "It . . . I couldn't get it to look right. I tried for a long time." He grins, then laughs out loud, takes a sip of his drink, seems utterly delighted. "Never mind," he says finally, still smiling. "You look fine. You look great, in fact. Let's forget about the hat." He leans forward and takes both of my hands between his, as if to warm them for a child who has come inside after building a snowman. "Don't be nervous," he says. "There is nothing to be nervous about."

A waiter appears, hovering two steps to one side of us. He orders wine for me, more scotch for himself, still in the same position: his elbows on his knees, shoulders hunched forward, his hands around mine. I sit stiffly, erect, my eyes on my arms stretched woodenly toward him. I am overcome by that mixture of contradictory feelings I should long be used to, since one variation or another has assaulted me almost daily since we've known each other. I am deeply embarrassed, I am flushed, I am shaking—and I am exhilarated, drunk before my wine arrives, ablaze with mindless gusto.

The waiter has no reaction at all, at least to judge from his expression when he brings our drinks and when I can finally bring myself to look up at him. "It's all inside you, you know," says the man sitting across from me, in the same suit that I'm wearing. "Nobody else ever cares. But it does make it a lot of fun for me that you do." We move on to a dining room then, where he holds my hand between courses. I have difficulty chewing, even more so swallowing; I drink close to twice the amount of wine

I'm used to. He has another drink at the bar, his hand loosely on my thigh.

Upstairs in the room he propels me toward the mirror. His arm around my shoulder, we look at our reflection: two men, one tall and clean-shaven, the shorter one sandy-bearded; dark suits, a pink shirt and a pale blue one. "Take your belt off," he says, in a low voice, and I do, unable to take my eyes from his in the mirror. Not knowing what to do next, I coil it into the tight serpent it had been in its box. He takes it from me, says "Get on the bed," and, "No, hands and knees." He reaches from behind me to open my trousers, then says, "Pull your pants down over your ass." Something gives way in me and my elbows can't hold my weight. On my knees, my head on my arms, sounds from my throat that I can't interpret: neither fear nor longing but the inability to distinguish between the two, adding up to . . . He beats me, a pillow over my head to muffle my cries, then takes me as he would a man. I cry out louder than before, my eyes wide open to the dark of the pillow covering my face. Deep inside me his pounding stops abruptly. He forces me down flat, his right hand under me and between my legs. Lying on top of me, stretched full length, he lifts the pillow, listens to my sobs subside. When I realize that we are breathing in unison, calmed, his fingers begin their infinitesimal move. Soon I am breathing rapidly again. He pushes the pillow back over my face when I come and soon he comes, too. He puts wadded Kleenex off the bedside table between my buttocks. It is soaked with semen and tinged pink when he removes it, later on. Curled against me, he murmurs, "So tight and hot, you can't imagine...."

SOMETIMES I WONDERED abstractly how it was possible that pain could be this exciting. Once during that time I stubbed my toe, in sandals, on my bottom desk drawer. I swore, hopped up and down, hobbled down the corridor to a co-worker's office to get sympathy from him, and couldn't concentrate on work for the next fifteen minutes because the slight but incessant throbbing distracted and annoyed me. But when he was the one inflicting pain, the difference between pain and pleasure became obscured in a way that turned them into two sides of a single coin: sensations different in quality but equal in result, equally intense, one stimulus as powerfully able as the next to arouse me. Since pain always came as a prelude and only then—sometimes hours earlier but always eventually leading to orgasm—it became as longed for, as sensuous, as integral to lovemaking as having my breasts caressed.

THERE IS A pounding at the front door. It's 6:30 P.M. and I've only just let myself in a few minutes earlier. When I peer past the chain lock, there he is: rolling his eyes, a bag of groceries in the crook of his right arm, the handle of his briefcase between thumb and index finger, the remaining fingers of his left hand curled around the top of a bag festooned with the Bendel's logo; the *Post*, folded lengthwise, is stuck between his teeth.

A decisive shake of his head—the newspaper swishes across celery tops—tells me he does not wish to be unburdened. He walks into the kitchen and sets the groceries down with a satisfying thump; makes a sharp turn, drops the *Post* in the hallway and his briefcase in the doorway to the bedroom. The briefcase clatters loudly. He winks at me gravely and with both hands, ceremoniously, deposits the Bendel's bag on the unmade bed. "*After* dinner," he says, to my raised eyebrow and grin. "You didn't carry the paper in your teeth on the street," I say. "No," he says. "I stuck it in my mouth just before I banged on the door, with my foot. For effect." He looks me sternly up and down.

"Now?" I ask, after the salad. "Certainly not," he says. "What do you think this is, Weight Watchers? We're having an omelette." "His Majesty can't think of what to cook. Again." He nods grimly: "And you'll love it." After the omelette is gone—his omelettes are luscious: crisp vegetables laced throughout, melted cheese on top, whole, sautéed mushrooms on the side—I clear my throat. "Now?" "Really," he says, "you'd think you've never eaten here before. Don't I usually manage some sort of dessert? There's baklava." *"Baklava,"* I groan, "after eggs, what a lurid combination, I'm full." "Please yourself," he says. "I've been tasting it ever since it leered at me from a greasy deli on Bleecker. You can watch me eat."

When I have slurped the last drops of honey off his fingers I smack my lips. "Disgusting," he says. "You look like you need another bath. There's stuff on your neck, for Christ's sake, even your eyebrows are sticky."

He gets a dripping washcloth and scrubs at my face. "All right," I say, pompously. "That's it. May I please see what's in the Bendel's bag?" "You never even *found* the *second* bag," he gloats. "I hid it inside the grocery bag, it bruised the tomatoes. Besides, I haven't had my coffee yet, I'll be liable to fall asleep without caffeine, it's been a long day."

It takes another fifteen minutes before we are ensconced in the living room. I am sitting on a pillow at the foot of the couch, handcuffed to the coffee table; waiting for him while he puts the coffee on, heats water for my tea, washes the dishes, carries the tray into the living room.

He makes a great show of being relaxed and content: lights a cigarette for me, swings his feet onto the table, stifles a yawn, reaches for the *Post*. I scream: "WHAT'S IN THE BENDEL'S BAG?"

He puts an index finger to his lower lip and knits his brow. "Shhhhh! Sh! How crass can you be? The rent's high on purpose here, to keep screamers out. Old lady Chrysler'll be at the door in a minute, did I tell you about her? Down the hall, in 15D. Needs to hear a new rape story every week and a couple of muggings, else she's plagued by irregularity. She's been short of juicy news nine days now...." "Making fun of elderly women's bodily functions," I say, "you can't get much lower than that. Next I'll kick the coffee table out from under you. That'll wrench your spine and cause long-term lower backache."

He sighs ostentatiously, swings his feet off

the table, disappears, and is back again in three leaps, a parcel in each hand, arms stretched triumphant above his head. He throws the packages across the room, kneels beside me to undo the handcuffs. He rubs my wrists automatically: a reflex that has become ingrained with him and has nothing to do with the condition of my wrists, which, this time as most times, show not even a pink line where the metal has touched them. I have become adept at staying comfortable and unscathed within them.

"O.K.," he says. "I'll sit down and you'll go over there and see what's in it and put it on."
"Fifteen B living theater," I mutter and he nods. "You bet. Command performance."

I open the Bendel's bag first. It contains, swathed in the throwaway luxury of six layers of tissue paper, a black lace garter belt and a pair of pale gray stockings. Seamed. Mirth rises irresistibly in my throat. I laugh out loud, laugh and laugh, hold the lace contraption stretched end to end high in the air—it looks vaguely skeletal and batlike. I put it on my head. I catch one dangling strap between my teeth, cross my eyes at the one that swings past my nose, a third tickles my ear. "Cornrows!" he bellows, "you've never looked so exotic...."
He yelps, he roars, he hoots. We are caught up, across the large room between us, in the kind of

fit one sometimes succumbs to as a child, without warning, during recess; or at a very specific, advanced, and brief stage of drunkenness: when it is impossible to explain the joke to a bystander; when it is impossible to explain the joke to oneself, not that one tries; when it is impossible to stop laughing, long after one's sides ache.

"What on earth..." He rubs his face and punches the cushion beside him. By the time he answers I've calmed down. I have pulled the thing off my head and hold it in my lap. "Look at it this way," he says, still smiling. "I'm catching up, pretty late, with an old fantasy of mine. Adolescent. Eleven, hell, that's not even...anyway. I've done so much stewing over these things—as an eleven-year-old, at fifteen, at twenty-two, at thirty-two. A *black garter belt*, not in a magazine, not in the movies, but on a *live woman*. And stockings with seams! And not a soul I've ever slept with wore them, not a one, so help me God. What can I tell you...I had to take matters into my own hands." He leers broadly and winks. "I finally want to see what it all looks like, in real life."

I've never worn a garter belt, I tell him, though I've thought about buying one, off and on for years. Except, I tell him, I can't remember ever imagining myself in black, that would have been...pink, maybe, or white; we're both laughing again. He describes the dignified saleswoman who waited on him, a woman our mothers' age: large-bosomed, impeccable, glistening-mouthed, coolly uninterested. She had spread a bewildering array before him and had pointed out salient features: adjustable straps; an elastic inset at the back of this one—better fit; special darts, here; small rosettes of contrasting fabric and color enhancing the snaps on yet another one; all, naturally, cold-water-washable. "You've chosen one of the two best-selling models, sir," she had told him. He had wanted to ask her what the other one was but had decided against it when she had said, "Will there be anything else?" in what had seemed to him a near-venomous voice.

"Now look in the other box," he says, gleefully, and pushes the low table away from the couch. He is sitting with his legs apart, bare feet planted on the carpet, toes pointing outward; an elbow on each knee, his chin in the palm of his hands, his two ring fingers rubbing the skin at the outer corners of his eyes. His hair, dry now from the shower he took before dinner, lies soft above his forehead. A fine white cotton shirt, heavily frayed at the collar, unbuttoned, sleeves rolled up, chest hair curly and lower down less curly, disappearing into old and baggy tennis shorts. "You don't know what you look like, right now," I say. "A Crusoe, happy on his island, who'll never wear a suit again, I'm so in love with you."

He narrows his eyes and catches his lower lip with an upper canine, trying to mask a grin— shy and pleased and so utterly dear to me that my vision blurs. He leans into the couch, head bent far back onto the cushions; his arched throat gleams across the room. He pushes both hands through his hair and says to the ceiling— evenly, deliberately—"This has got to go on like this. All we have to do is just make it go on like this." And sitting up and hunching forward and waving an outstretched arm and pointed finger at me, in a booming voice: "Open the other bag, damn it, you wheedled and whined all evening, now look at you drag your feet!"

"All *right*," I say, "yes, *sir*!" The bag contains a shoe box from Charles Jourdan, a store I've only looked at from outside, acknowledging wisely that even my Bloomingdale's card is at times too much of a temptation. I lift the shiny beige lid. Swaddled in yet more tissue paper lies a pair of elegant, light gray suede pumps with heels so high I'm appalled. "*You* walk in these," I say, vehemently. "My *God*, I didn't even know they made heels like that." He ambles across the room and crouches beside me on the floor, grinning sheepishly.

"Yeah, well, I see what you mean." "See what I *mean*," I repeat. "How can you *not*, you're sure these are supposed to be shoes?" "They're shoes all right," he says. "I guess you don't like them. Not at all? I mean, aside from the heels?" "Sure," I say, holding one shoe in each hand, the suede soft as velvet. "What's not to like, they're sensational. Course, it's hard to overlook such outlandish appendages, probably cost a fortune, too...." He shrugs, suddenly awkward.

"Look," he says, "they're not really to wear, outside that is." He gestures at the Bendel's wrappings. "They're just for us. Me, really. Both of us. I wish you...what I mean is...but if you really hate them..." All at once he is a decade my junior, a very young man asking me to have a drink with him, expecting to be refused. I have not seen him like this before. "Darling," I say, overcome, in a rush, "they're lovely, feel this leather, of course I'll wear them...." "I'm glad," he says, with a remaining trace of sheepishness. "I was hoping you would; there's always a chance you might get to like them." And buoyant again: "Put the stuff on."

So I do. As always until this evening—and tonight for the last time—I am wearing only a shirt, so it doesn't take long, though getting the seams straight is much trickier than I would have guessed. The shoes fit perfectly. "I took your black ones with me," he says. "And I insisted and they found a girl that size and she tried on nine pairs before I settled on these. Thank God you're an average size."

The heels make me so much taller we're nearly eye to eye. He hugs me lightly, runs his hands up my sides to my breasts, moves the palm of each hand, fingers extended, in small circles, a nipple at the center of each. His face is blank. The gray pupils on which mine are focused reflect two miniature faces. His hands move down my midriff to the garter belt. He traces its outlines around my body, then, one by one, follows each of the four straps down to where the stockings begin. It is almost dark. He switches on the floor lamp behind us, says, "Stay there," walks back to the couch, and sits down. "Now," he says, in a husky voice, "come over here. Take your time."

I walk slowly across the carpet. I take small steps, cautious, my body tilted into a foreign alignment. My arms hang awkwardly from their sockets. Something roars in my ears, amplifying each breath I take.

"Turn around now," he says when I'm a few steps away from the couch. I can barely hear him. "And lift up the shirt." I turn and stand very straight, holding the shirttails tucked up at my sides with my elbows. "Are you disappointed?" I say, in what turns out to be a high-pitched, flat voice. "Are you kidding, you're a sight," he murmurs behind me, "you're a sight, sweetheart." My eyes close. I listen to the roar in my ears, every square inch of my skin aching to be touched. Trying to clear my ears, I shake my head, hair catches in my mouth; please, I think, please.

"Get down on all fours," he says. "And pull your shirt up. Pull it up, I want to see your ass." I look at the tightly woven carpet, a rich gray, now only a few inches from my face. "Crawl around," he says, his voice very low. "Crawl over to the door. Crawl around." I move my right arm forward, my right knee, my left arm. I think: is it elephants that do this differently? My left knee. I am suspended in a silence that is broken by someone's muffled conversation in the corridor outside the apartment. A door slams. The cellist on the floor below begins to practice and I concentrate on his characteristic initial outburst with interest. I have always assumed that musicians warm up slowly, like joggers. This one starts out with great verve and volume and gradually winds down over the course of his three-hour run. He is bald and surly, I've seen him in the elevator. "I can't," I say.

It seems as if the sound of my voice has made my body crumple. For a second my face is flat against the carpet, which appears flawlessly smooth when seen from a standing height but is less soft to the skin than one might expect. I sit up. The height of these heels prevents me from sitting in the position I suddenly long for: my knees drawn up to my chin, my arms around me.

"Tell me," he says, neutrally. "I feel stupid," I say. "It makes me feel foolish." The one lamp at the other end of the room is not bright enough for me to be able to see the expression on his face. He folds his arms behind his head and leans back against the couch cushions. I get up, teeter, say, "This rug itches"—under my breath, but as if imparting valuable information—and sit down in the nearest chair. I cross my arms over the shirtfronts I have wrapped around me. One of the sleeves has come down and I tug the cuff over my fingers and curl my hand, inside the fabric, into a fist.

"It's not as if we haven't been through all this," he says, not looking at me. "I hate packing. I hate unpacking even worse. It took me a week to unpack that suitcase of yours, the last time around." The cello below erupts as if flayed by a madman.

"What I don't get is why you can't keep the idea of being hit in your mind, why it always actually has to be done to you. Before you say to me, no, I don't want to do that—why you don't picture me taking off my belt, in your head. Why you don't remember from one night to the next what it feels like when it comes down on you. We have to fucking negotiate each and every time and in the end you do what I tell you, anyway."

"No," I say, inaudibly first. "No," I say, "please . . ." He leans toward me now, pushing hair off his forehead. "It makes me feel like a dog," I say, "crawling. . . . I'm scared you'll make fun of me."

"You *should* feel stupid," he says. "What a crock of shit. If I ever make fun of you I'll let you know." I shake my head, mute. Scowling and scrutinizing me closely, he walks toward and past me. I am sitting rigidly at the edge of the chair, my knees pressed together, my forearms tight against my stomach muscles. His hands are on my shoulders. I am pulled back until my shoulder blades touch the upholstery. Then his hand in my hair, massaging my scalp, closing into a fist, drawing slowly back until my face lies horizontal, the top of my head against his cock. He rubs the lower half of my face with the heel of his hand. My mouth soon opens. When I am moaning steadily he leaves the room and comes back with the riding crop. He lays it on the coffee table.

"Look at it," he says. "Look at me. In three

minutes I can get you so you'll be in bed for a week." But I barely hear him. The inadequate, the minuscule, the fiber optics passage I have in my throat instead of a trachea allows me only quicksilver sips of air. My open mouth feels bruised.

"Crawl," he says. I'm on hands and knees again. I press my face hard into my right shoulder and feel how the trembling in my chin, instead of being steadied, transmits through bone after bone until my arms shake and my legs, down to my toes. I hear the tip of the leather-covered handle scrape against the tabletop. A white-hot pain leaps across the back of my thighs. Tears spring to my eyes, sudden as magic. Released as if from a dangerous stupor, I crawl from the chair to the bedroom door, limber and easily to the lamp in the far corner; a loudly purring cat weaves figure eights around my arms. Both stockings tear at the knees and I can feel a run creep jerkily up each thigh. When I've almost reached the couch again he overtakes me, pushes me down, turns me on my back.

It's the one time with him and the first time at all that I come at the same time as my lover. He licks my face then. Each spot is first warm and—when his tongue moves on—abruptly cold, sweat and saliva evaporating in the conditioned air.

When he stops I open my eyes. "But you beat me anyway," I whisper, "even when I do what you..." "Yes," he says. "Because you like hitting me," I whisper. "Yes," he says, "and watching you flinch, and holding you down and hearing you beg. I love the sounds when you can't keep quiet, when you're past holding back. I love seeing a bruise on you and knowing where it came from, welts on your ass." I shiver. He reaches back and up and yanks down the old blanket he keeps folded under a cushion in the corner of the couch. He shakes it open and covers me with it and says, tucking the frayed satin binding under my chin, "And because you want it, too." "I do," I whisper. "Never *then*...never while..." "I know," he says, close to my ear, his hands deep in my hair, tight and soothing on my scalp.

No one saw my body except for him, a kid named Jimmy, and a woman whose name I wasn't told. Sometimes in the bathtub or when I caught my reflection in the mirror, I would regard my bruises with the unfocused curiosity reserved for looking at snapshots of other people's cousins. They had nothing to do with me. My body had nothing to do with me. It was a decoy, to be used whichever way he decided, toward the end of exciting us both.

WHILE UNDRESSING ME in preparation for my bath he says, "I've hired a masseur for tonight." He drops my blouse onto the white tiles of the bathroom floor. I step out of my skirt and sit on the edge of the tub while he takes off my shoes, then stand up again while he slips down my underpants. He likes my underpants—white cotton, Woolworth's. He likes this skirt, too; pulling it carefully up over my thighs this morning, he said, "That's my favorite skirt on you, does your ass justice." I watch him lean over the tub, push the plug; reach out to pick, after a moment's hesitation, a brightly printed packet wedged between the bottles lined up on the inside ledge of the tub. He leans forward again to turn on the water, tests its temperature, adjusts the left knob, and sprinkles green powder carefully under the gushing faucets.

It suddenly occurs to me how out of place he looks: a man in a well-fitted business suit, his tie sitting properly between two starched collar points, as if he were about to address a conference table, or speak into a news camera, or listen to yet another story of marital discord in preparation for court. Doing none of the things for which he is dressed, but leaning over a steaming bathtub instead, one hand braced at the edge of the porcelain, the other fingering the rapidly rising foam.

He sniffs: "Not bad, is it? A little sweet maybe, not quite as drenched-in-herbs as they rave on the package, but nice, anyway." I nod. He smiles at me so full of warmth, of bliss even, that something catches in my throat: all one could ever wish for is a small room filling with steam and the smell of lavender above an undercurrent of mint.

He leaves and comes back with the handcuffs. He fastens them around the wrists I stretch toward him and holds on to my elbow as I step into the water, which is on the verge of being too hot but will, I know, be perfect the moment I'm stretched out in it.

The tub is deep and three-quarters filled and I have to tilt my chin up to keep the bubbles out of my mouth. Only when he has turned off the water and glanced at me once more does he loosen his tie and take off his coat.

I hear him rummage in the kitchen, his footsteps sharp on the tiles, then muffled on the

living room carpet.... SHARED THE SECRETS OF
MY SOUL...Kris Kristofferson glides across
slopes of foam. We have listened to WQXR
only once since I have mentioned in passing,
during the course of God-knows-which forgotten conversation, that the station now playing
is my favorite. He had told me that an obscure
Vivaldi was scheduled that he had never heard.
"You don't need to *explain*," I had wailed,
"change the station, it's *your apartment*!" He
had grinned and winked at me and said, "I
know," and later decided that it hadn't been
first-rate Vivaldi but well worth listening to,
nonetheless.

...EVERY NIGHT SHE KEPT ME FROM THE
COLD...He comes back with a glass of Chablis,
squats beside the tub, tilts the glass for me to
drink from with his right hand...TRADE ALL
MY TOMORROWS FOR A SINGLE YESTERDAY
...pushing bubbles off my chin with his left.
The wine is ice-cold on my tongue...HOLDING
BOBBY'S BODY NEXT TO MINE...

He settles back on the toilet and unbuttons
his vest with one hand, takes three long gulps.
"His name's Jimmy. He sounded Irish on the
phone. Did you ever hear of an Irish masseur?"
"No," I say and giggle...FREEDOM'S JUST
ANOTHER WORD FOR..."I thought they were all
Swedish."...NOTHIN' LEFT TO LOSE..."I did
too," he says, "or possibly French."...NOTHIN'

AIN'T WORTH NOTHIN'... "What is he coming here for?"... BUT IT'S FREE... "To do a tap dance on the kitchen counter, pretty stupid question there."... FEELIN' GOOD WAS EASY, LORD... "That massage you had that you told me about,"... FEELIN' GOOD WAS GOOD ENOUGH FOR ME... "I thought you'd like another one."

I think, yes, that's it. I can't ever just say something—anything—and consider it forgotten. He pays attention to what I say, it's hard to get used to, you don't often run across such a peculiar habit. There is nothing that merely amuses or interests him at the moment, he always draws consequences. If I'm looking at *Newsweek* and read a passage from a book review out loud, he will buy the book for me that week. In the middle of an hours-long rambling and partly drunk conversation on a Saturday night he describes picking blueberries behind his aunt's house where he stayed for a summer at the age of nine, and I say, "Blueberries, don't you love blueberries." About midnight he says, "I'm going to get the paper." Half an hour later there he is, carrying the *Times* all right under one arm, but in the other he has a brown paper bag and inside is a container of blueberries. He washes and hulls and drains them while I read the Arts and Leisure section. And he's bought a pint of heavy cream and pours a greedy heap of berries into a large salad bowl and feeds them to me until I say, "If I have one more spoonful I'm going to be sick," and he grins and eats the few leftover berries floating in cream. "Where on earth did you get these at this hour?" I finally think to ask. "Grew them," he says solemnly, "on the corner of Sixth and Greenwich," and slurps the remaining liquid loudly, holding the bowl with both hands.

The masseur arrives at five to eight. He looks about twenty. He is short and stocky, with a great deal of wavy blond hair and bulging biceps under a dark blue T-shirt and nylon jacket. He wears jeans and sneakers and carts one towel and a bottle of oil in an Icelandic flight bag. I take off my shirt as I'm told and lie on my stomach on the bed. "I'm going to watch," he announces to the silent Jimmy. "I'd like to learn what you do, so I can do it when you're not available." "Always available," grunts Jimmy and dive-bombs onto my shoulders. His hands, slick with oil, are much larger than one would expect from someone his height—huge and warm. My arms turn limp, I have to fight to keep my mouth from lolling open. His palms work their way up my rib cage, slowly, digging deeply, a steady advance. My shoulders again, another start at the waist. I am close to grunting whenever his hands bear down. "Let me try it," his voice above me. The big hands lifted. My eyelids as heavy as if shut under water. These hands are cooler, touching me lightly by comparison. The masseur corrects him wordlessly, demonstrates, then the cool hands on me again with more weight this time. The big paws on my thighs, bypassing the towel across my buttocks. My calves next, then my feet. Teacher and pupil in turn grasping a foot with one hand, applying exquisite pressure with the other. I'm turned over. The process reverses up the front of my body. I am long past containing myself and groan blissfully under the bear arms that grind me into the sheets. He repeats each of the masseur's moves, now much less tentatively, close in effect to what the monster hands do. My muscles are ablaze and suspended. It's over. Someone covers me with a sheet and turns off the lights.

I hear the giddy, whooshing sound a nylon sleeve makes when an arm is pushed into it. The refrigerator door slams. Two beer cans pop. For a while there is mumbling, which lulls me further. I am almost asleep. "... Twenty-five extra." The bedside lamp is lit again. I am told to lie across the width of the bed, face down. The sheet is thrown over my legs. I hear the squeak of the closet door, the explosive crack of a fresh sheet being shaken free of its laundry creases; cool cotton slides across my shoulders and back. A belt is being unbuckled. There is the grating of leather pulled sharply through cloth loops.

The skin on the back of my body is divided into distinct segments. The areas that have been massaged are subdued, smoothed to a trance under the sheets. The skin now exposed bristles with tension, a faint draft from the air conditioner sluicing each capillary.

"What is it, Jimmy?" There is a growl. "You got the wrong man." More throat-clearing. "You don't understand"; his voice is smooth. "I told you, you're not going to hurt her, I promise you. You don't see her struggling, do you? Is she yelling for the neighbors? It makes her hot, I'm telling you, that's what she gets off on." "So *you* hit her." "Thirty, then." The mattress gives under the weight of a body that settles to my right. I am struck a few times and bury my head in the crook of an elbow.

"At that rate you'll be here forever." His voice is very close to my head, there is the odor of beer and sweat. The mattress moves under me again as the body to my right shifts its weight. A hand is in my hair and my head is pulled up. I open my eyes. "Thirty-five." The blows fall harder. He is crouching on the floor beside the bed. Our faces almost touch. The whites of his eyes are laced with red, his pupils are dilated. I can't keep from wincing now and begin to squirm. "Forty," he says, in a low voice. His forehead glistens. The body above me braces a knee in the middle of my back and under the next blow my mouth opens wide. I struggle silently, trying to pry his fist from my hair with one hand, pushing his face away from me with the other, thrashing my legs. He forces my wrists together, holds them in a fierce lock, resumes his grip in my hair, yanks up my head. "Come on, you bastard, fifty," he hisses and covers my mouth with his. The blow that follows makes me moan inside his mouth, under the next one I wrench free and cry out. "That's enough, Jimmy," he says, as if to a waiter who has served him too large a portion, or to a child who is having a minor tantrum at the end of a tiring day.

THROUGHOUT THE ENTIRE PERIOD, the daytime rules of my life continued as before: I was independent, I supported myself (to the extent of my lunches, at any rate, and of keeping up an empty apartment, gas and phone bills at a minimum), came to my own decisions, made my choices. The nighttime rules decreed that I was helpless, dependent, totally taken care of. No decisions were expected of me, I had no responsibilities. I had no choice.

I loved it. I loved it, I loved it, I loved it, I loved it.

From the minute I closed his front door behind me, there was nothing more for me to do, I was there to be done to. Someone else had taken control of my life, down to the last detail. If control was out of my hands, I, in turn, was allowed to be out of control. For weeks on end I was flooded by an overwhelming sense of relief at being unburdened of adulthood. "Would you let me blindfold you?" had been the first and last question of any importance asked of me. From then on, nothing was ever again a matter of my assent or protest (though once or twice my qualms became part of the process: to make my addiction clear to me); of my weighing priorities or alternatives—practical, intellectual, moral; of considering consequences. There was only the voluptuous luxury of being a bystander to one's own life; an absolute relinquishing of individuality; an abandoned reveling in the abdication of self-hood.

I WAKE UP not feeling right. It isn't any better after breakfast and by eleven o'clock it is worse. By lunchtime I feel thoroughly chilled. I order a cardboard container of chicken soup to eat at my desk, but the first spoonful is like rancid oil on my tongue and I cannot bring myself to take another one. By three in the afternoon I decide this isn't a passing discomfort. I tell the receptionist I am ill and go home—to my apartment.

I barely manage to push the door shut behind me. A stagnant smell closes in on me. The apartment is stifling hot. Dust particles dance before locked windows, the mirror above the fireplace iridescent in the vicious glare. I crawl onto the bed, shivering uncontrollably but unable to get under the covers. I tug at the bedspread beneath me and finally grab hold of a loose end, which I pull over my shoulders. The sun shines directly onto my face, which feels as if about to burst into flames. As soon as I lift my head off the pillow in an effort to get up and draw the shades, I become too dizzy to keep my eyes open.

The telephone wakes me from a nightmare that has me consumed by hordes of outsized fire ants. I push off the bedspread and bring the receiver to my ear without opening my eyes. "What's wrong?" he says. "I must be coming down with something," I mutter, feeling as cold now as if sprawled on ice instead of no-iron cotton polyester. "I'll be right over," he says. The phone clicks, then hums. "Don't," I say and put the hand that holds the receiver onto my chest. I am really sick, I think, visualizing the word through the gyroscope inside my forehead. I'm never sick, I think, and in the middle of summer, that's the most ridiculous, the most...

This time I am awakened by the doorbell. I do not move. It rings, in staccato bursts, again and again. Finally the noise seems worse than getting up. I make it to the door without once opening my eyes. While I keep saying, "I want to stay here," he picks me up, kicks the door shut behind him, and carries me to the elevator. "I can't stand people when I'm sick, I hate to have them around," I mumble into his neck. "I have to be sick in my own bed," I finally say, in as loud a voice as I can muster. "Not *that* sick," he says, holding me propped upright in the elevator. I am too dizzy to answer. He half-carries, half-drags me to the waiting cab. There is a mess of arms and legs and another trip to another elevator and then I'm in the bed I know better than my own by now, undressed this time and one of his shirts on me.

Through a haze he says, "I'm going out to buy a thermometer." Cold glass in my mouth after a while and then not and then his voice on the phone.

A hand shakes my shoulder. "This is . . . friend of mine, still makes housecalls." A pink-cheeked man looms above me, beaming square, oil-slicked teeth that rearrange themselves incessantly and with terrifying speed. A tongue depressor in my mouth, someone probing. Later his voice again, ". . . getting stuff at the drugstore," and then pills to swallow. I still intend to explain how I want no one around me when I'm sick, have been adamant about this since adolescence. But my body aches too badly and it doesn't seem to matter enough, just then, to warrant the effort.

I wake up to a dim room, the bedside alarm clock saying 4:00. My muscles ache even worse than before but at least I'm no longer dizzy. "They call that sleeping around the clock," he says, from the doorway. "I'm glad you're up, you have to take some more pills." "What do you keep giving me?" I say. "Stuff Fred prescribed. You've got the flu." "What are you doing here?" I say and he grins. "I live here." I am too weak to banter. "Why aren't you at work?" "I called in," he says. "For you, too. You need somebody home for a couple of days." "No, I don't," I say, but even in mid-sentence I know very well that yes, I do need someone with me, and yes, he is right to stay home with me, and yes, I need to be taken care of. I say no more and neither does he.

He stayed home the next day and the morning of the next. I was in bed for five days, then spent the weekend taking naps and sitting on the living room couch. He bought a bed tray—an elaborate thing, painted white, with legs and a compartment on the side for newspapers, and a shelf part that slants up on hinges like a music stand. He fed me aspirin and antibiotics. He concocted a brew that I drank for three days before asking what it was; it turned out to be a third each apricot juice, grapefruit juice, and rum, heated to just below boiling. I sat, propped against the headboard, in his air-conditioned bedroom, July sizzling outside as if on another continent. Inside, the shades were drawn; his ski sweater over my shoulders, I drank steaming yellow stuff, sleeping well after each eight-ounce mug. Later, soups, then milk shakes he got at the corner, alternating vanilla and strawberry;

finally our regular meals according to his rotating calendar. By then I was awake for longer periods of time. My head was clear, though my body still felt as if it had been dropped from a great height. He lugged the TV into the bedroom and put the remote control on the pillows next to mine. And a heap of magazines. In the evenings he sat on the chair next to the bed and told me gossip he had self-consciously amassed by taking one of my colleagues to lunch, then read the paper aloud. He taught me to play poker and let me win. He slept on the living room couch.

I had not been nursed this way since having the chicken pox at the age of eight.

TODAY IS THE last day for me to come up with a present for my mother's birthday with any hope of getting it to her on time. It is a sweltering Saturday. One would not, however, suspect that it is ninety degrees outside: the air in Saks is chilled to a crisp, swarming, wallowing hordes of customers notwithstanding. We are bent over one of the jewelry counters, fingering lockets and thin gold chains. I have narrowed the choice down to a heart-shaped one and one that opens to reveal a minute bouquet of hand-painted forget-me-nots, when he whispers, "Steal it." I bolt upright, upsetting the heap of packages that the woman next to me has wedged between the front of the counter and one raised thigh. His back is moving away from me in the throng.

My ears burn as if to set my hair afire. I wait for the blood to recede from my face. I watch a vein pulse in my left hand lying on the counter, I lose track of the vein and look at my hand instead: it has closed over the heart-shaped locket.

The saleswoman stands two feet to my right. Three customers are talking to her at once. There are circles under her eyes and the skin around her smile is tight. It's not fair to steal on a Saturday, says a small voice in my head. Look at her: she's clutching the edge of the counter as if under siege, she's tired, she's especially tired of being polite; she would happily shout at us all: give me a break! get lost! let me go home! What a rotten thing to do, says the small voice, at least you could pick a Tuesday morning, and why you went all these years without pocketing a left-behind dime in a pay phone only to start shoplifting at this stage of your life . . . I pick up the second locket in my right hand, and the nearest gold chain, and say loudly, in the saleswoman's direction, "I'll take these, may I have these, please." She smiles at me and says, "That one's my favorite too."

I fumble with my charge plate, sign the receipt, snatch at the paper bag. . . . He is leaning against a bus stop sign across Fiftieth Street. He waves to me and simultaneously raps at the window of a cab just then sliding past him. He waits, holding the back door open, until I have crossed the street and sit in the far seat, gets in, gives his address to the driver, and gloats: "Pretty fair timing, if I say so myself, and air-conditioned, too." Only then does he hold out an open palm in my direction. I drop the locket—slippery wet from my fist—onto dry skin. "I bought another one," I say. "I couldn't just leave...." He laughs, ruffles my hair with one hand, pulls me toward him with the other. My head comes to rest on his chest. His shirt feels crisp. His skin smells as immaculately of soap as if he'd just had a shower. "That wasn't quite what I had in mind," he says, "but it'll do." And in mock bewilderment, "Are you *shaking*?" He holds me tightly.

He is pleased with me, but so matter-of-fact and at ease that I think: he knew all along that I'd do it, he never had a doubt. I turn my head until my face is buried under his arm and close my eyes. It took no time at all, I think, and very little effort, really; a lark.

As soon as we get home he addresses an envelope, wraps the locket and its $39.95 price tag in several layers of toilet paper, and sticks a stamp on the envelope. "Run down to the lobby and mail this, there's a good girl. They should have it back by Tuesday." I stare at him, then at the envelope. He snaps his fingers: "You know what we forgot? Wrapping paper for your mother's locket, why didn't you have it giftwrapped? I'll go get some at the drugstore and by the time I'm back I hope you'll have that silly look off your face. You didn't exactly crack Fort Knox, sweetheart, remember?"

A few days later he shows me the loveliest knife I have ever seen. I am sitting on his lap when he pulls it out of the inside pocket of his suit jacket. Its handle is silver, inlaid in mother-of-pearl. He shows me how to make the blade snap out of its sheath with a frivolous click, how to make the shiny steel disappear again between silver scrollwork. "Do you want to try it?" The slim handle lies in my palm, cool and precise and as well known to me as if I had received it years ago, as a gift: to herald the age of consent.

I hand the lovely object back reluctantly. He slips it open once more, lays the tip of the blade very lightly against the skin of my throat. I bend my neck back, back some more, back until it will not bend any farther. The steel tip feels harmless—a toothpick. "Don't laugh," he says, "It'll go right through..." but I do laugh and he has known I would and has long moved the toothpick out of the way by the time I burst out giggling. "I withdrew this knife point in the nick of time," he says. "Nick of time, get it?" "You make the worst jokes of any man I've ever met," I say, in a guttural voice, my head still arched toward my back. "Don't try to arouse me with tales of your former lovers," he says. "It's so tacky. Only trash does that." "That's

me," I say, "showing my true colors at last."
"True colors at last," he says, "what insufferable arrogance, as if I didn't know what you were the minute I laid eyes on you." "Oh, yeah?" I say, sitting up. "Oh, yeah?" I'm at a loss of what to say next, but I need not have worried. He interrupts my fumbling, half-grown, incoherent scraps of thought and says, "Next week you'll rob somebody. In an elevator would be easiest, you can dress up in your Bluebeard outfit, don't tell me about it in advance. Now get off my lap, my legs won't wake up for three days as it is."

I know immediately which elevator. I have often picked up a friend of mine for lunch, at her office down two blocks from mine. I know that the second floor in her company's building has been vacant for months, its door to the stairwell unlocked. The following day I have an appointment at three. It is over within half an hour and I take the subway to his apartment instead of going back to my office. It's a humid day and the ride back uptown is uncomfortable. How can they stand being dressed like this, I think, in the middle of July. I am sweating in shirt and vest and suit jacket, women in sleeveless dresses looking airy to me and as if in flight. I finger the smooth oblong in my pocket, expecting instructions to flow from it as from a talisman-guidebook.

I have, on several occasions, exchanged nods with this doorman. That he does not recognize me makes me feel invisible and giddy. I stand before the board listing the names and suite numbers of the companies in the building, glancing sideways at the people to my left: two women are waiting in front of the banks of elevators leading to the upper floors, a middle-aged man before those for the lower floors. I walk toward the opening doors of one of the elevators serving floors one through eighteen.

Three men and one woman emerge and file past the middle-aged man and me. I step into the elevator after him. He presses 9. I push 2. Even before the doors have closed, the slim silver handle is out of my pocket. The playful click coincides with the onset of our ascent. There's the tip of the switchblade at his throat, which arches backward at an angle familiar to me. I hold out my free hand. A leather wallet—still warm—lies in my palm just as the doors open. I stand outside. We look at each other, somber as in a turn-of-the-century photograph, until the doors slide shut. Neither of us has spoken. I walk ten steps to the stairwell, down one flight, through a gray metal door into the lobby. The doorman is drinking from a Styrofoam cup and exchanging jokes with the afternoon mailman. I walk past them and out the revolving door and two blocks to the subway and up the subway steps a few miles farther south, and four blocks to his apartment.

There's enough time for me to undress and put my own clothes back on and scrub the glue off my face before he comes home. I am sitting on the couch, pretending to read the evening paper. He says, "Early, aren't you," and, "I bought a porterhouse, the damn thing's worth its weight in gold." I do not look up from the print, which blurs before my eyes. A delayed reaction has set in: I need to make a concentrated effort to keep from sobbing, and I am trying to understand why my thighs ache, why muscles deep inside my vagina are opening up and out, why I am aroused as if his tongue were goading me toward air that is dangerously thin and piercing.

The newspaper slides into my lap without a rustle. He has discovered the wallet on the coffee table. "Ah . . ." he says and puts down his briefcase. "Open it."

Open it . . . open . . . open it: my body interprets the words as having nothing to do with the wallet. I slip off the couch and kneel before the low table. He sits behind me, rubbing my neck and shoulders. I take out, one by one, a small address book, a checkbook, an American Express card, a Diner's Club card, a Master

Charge card; a driver's license, a thin, black, refillable pencil, a crumpled scrap of paper with two phone numbers scrawled in ballpoint; a florist's card, a mortician's card, a classified ad torn from the *Village Voice* offering cut-rate carpentry services, a pink receipt from a Third Avenue dry cleaner, and three hundred and twenty-one dollars.

"Hm," he says. His chin rests on my right shoulder now. His left arm is curled around me, his palm caresses my breasts. His right arm—slipped between my rib cage and my right elbow—stretches before me toward the table-top, where it lines up the contents of the wallet in an orderly row.

"Leonard Burger, August 14, 1917," he reads off the driver's license into my ear. "What a clever name they gave him—our Leo's a leo. Unless he's just a Len. But what do you make of the mortician's card? And why the carpenter? Was he pricing coffins, got discouraged with a seller's market and decided to trust a drummer on dope who's handy with a saw? Or does he just need new kitchen cabinets . . . ?" He tells me to call the numbers off the rumpled piece of paper, hands me the phone: one is busy and stays busy, there's no answer at the second.

"This is losing its charm," he says. "Call Len. Leo. Tell him his wallet's in the trash down the street. . . ." "Here?" I say. "You want him to come here?" "It'll be fun to watch." "We don't know his number," I say, my voice unfamiliar to me, my composure in the elevator unfathomable in retrospect. He points to the first page of the address book. PLEASE RETURN TO, it says, and then there's his name, an address, and below that a telephone number. A woman answers. "Mr. Burger's wallet is at the corner of..." She says, "What?" in a high-pitched voice, and, "Who...?" but he has motioned me to hang up. "I give him half an hour," he says and leaves the room to start my bath. The salad is prepared and the table set when he leads me back to the living room window.

We stand next to each other. His hand follows the shape of my buttocks over and over. A little yellow car pulls up to the curb, miles below us. A tiny man scrambles out. The toy car zips away while the toy man scurries toward a pretend garbage can. "Try this," he says in a low voice, into my ear, and when I look at him he grins and hands me his field glasses. A CinemaScope face, drawn and gray, looms inches from mine. I recognize the wart on the left cheek, large beads of sweat glisten on a heavily lined forehead. One earlobe, a gray sprig of hair protruding from the cavity above, looks, incongruously, as if it had once been pierced.

He has hidden the wallet under only one

layer of newspaper. "What if someone else finds it first?" I had asked. "Too bad for Leonard." But no one has taken the wallet, there is no need even to forage. Spidery-veined giant's hands hover, gingerly lift a vast sports page, a Spandex watchband catches the low sun. I put the glasses down. The toy man snatches up a grain of dust, stands immobile, swivels its head, waves a tiny arm at a little model Checker, and is gone.

A wave of nausea rises from the pit of my stomach. I swallow hard. The sour taste lasts only for a moment. I stretch my arms as far above my head as they will go and find—as my shoulder muscles respond to the pull, and the band of muscles across my chest, and the stomach muscles below—that a shifting, a sliding has begun in my body while I was still afraid of throwing up. The stir gathers momentum and depth, embracing small rivulets, now plentiful from all sides. He spins me around, his hands steel clamps on my shoulders, and shakes me, my head bobbing. His hands close around my throat, I slide to the floor, my eyes shut. I lower my circle of arms joined at the wrists around his neck and entwine my ankles above the middle of his back.

"Barely worth it, wouldn't you say?" He grins down at me over a forkful of steak. "A

Candid Camera stunt's livelier." But his eyes shine as if he had a low-grade fever and I don't need to wonder whether mine do too.

I HAD NEVER allowed anyone to read my diaries. They had been a fitful business, sometimes carried on intently in lurching subway cars (one hand shielding the page from passengers standing above me, self-conscious sidelong glances at those touching my thighs to the right and left); equally self-conscious at my desk, between a hurried return from a demonstration with a client and a staff meeting scheduled fifteen minutes later; or alone at night, a foot away from a mute and bright three-inch Kojak running heavily down a windy street, his crook of the evening sliding around a corner, garbage cans silently sent sprawling on sidewalks; or in locked bathrooms, crouched on a cold toilet cover, water left running in the sink so as not to let on to the man in my bed that I was writing: "This is getting to be...I used to want...long over-due..."; daily entries obsessive for months, then neglected for no clear reason for half a year except for sporadic sentences, "March 8, raining, hair wretched."

I had always been wary of people who published their diaries. It seemed a violation to me to have a true diary read publicly, and a diary written to be read by others—having lost its purpose: to be one's secret place—could at heart be no more than variations on "March 8, raining, hair wretched."

Some years back I had surprised a lover holding my open diary. Though I knew he could scarcely have read a word, so short a time had I been gone from the room; though I knew he was unhappy at how things stood between us and had maybe hoped for a clue; though I knew that my leaving him over the diary would not be to the point, the incident clearly a pretext even to me—still I thought, that's it, this does it. I said nothing and watched him close the book awkwardly. I left, and for weeks thought of him only in terms of half a sentence: "... reading my diary, too."

Since I had met him I had written every day, three or four sentences at first, soon pages and pages. When he picked up the diary one evening out of my open briefcase next to the coffee table, and began to leaf through it, a curious mix of sensations rose up my spine: dismay at first; then relief, enchantment, exultation. How had I been able to bear it? All the times when he hadn't read this notebook, how long had it been, there had been no one to read me. An adolescent's code, a dense scribbling complicated by a smattering of leftover Latin, meant to be indecipherable to anyone but me—and sometimes beyond even me, mere weeks later. All the times of rushing to bureau drawers when the doorbell rang, sliding notebooks under slips and handkerchiefs; all the times of last-minute looks around a room to make sure something I didn't want seen, something I wanted no one to know about, hadn't been left exposed. Always to be laden with recesses not to be opened to anyone; the grim isolation, the bleakness of privacy. Over, I thought, it's over, he knows me completely, there is nothing to hide, and sat down at the foot of the couch and watched him read.

JUST CALLED HIM at work, reassuring to hear the receptionist's voice recite a company name, then croon, "Just a moment please." Reassuring to hear his secretary answer half a minute later, reassuring to listen to her say, ". . . may be out to lunch, if he is he didn't tell me, may I take a message?" I need reassurance. Left the office at ten-thirty, no appointments for the rest of the day, planning to get caught up on backlog working at home; and now this, instead.

He calls back. "We're an anachronism," I whisper, reading from the dictionary into the phone in a raspy voice; nearly every one of the definitions incorporates the word "error." "It's not normal to wander around a man's apartment on a Monday afternoon, obsessed." One cup of syrupy coffee nursed for hours, chain-smoking, time slipping away. "I'm scared." And why not, I think, even as I whisper into the phone, my bridges burning behind me in bright rows, signposts of what I've abandoned for him: a comprehensive—if secondhand—grid of a code: *how*one*lives*, assembled over decades. Eyes looking ahead, open wide as in a trance, no idea yet what I'm looking at. There's cause for alarm all right, it would be abnormal to be whistling through my days. The responses are correct, well-oiled brain/well-scrutinized emotional machinery ticking away in unison, all in gear. New events, not enough information available, are liable to be unsettling; new sequences more unsettling than isolated events, new processes more alarming yet. . . .

"Anachronism," he repeats after me, and there is a pause, and then he says lightly, "So maybe we are and so who cares. We're fine." "Tell me what to do," I say. "Maybe you should go back to the office," he says. "Do office work at the office. Or give it until three. If you're not working by then, you'll know."

He's set my afternoon out for me, it's crisp and clear, divided into segments, so much for that, thirty minutes on that, no more pacing from room to room. I'll do what he says. I'll do what he tells me, forever. Too big a word, better stay away from those, you ought to know better. But what if I've found an absolute after all? Always, never, forever, completely: I'll always love him, I'll love him completely,

I'll never stop, I'll do what he tells me forever—
how stern a theology can you pick? The god of
wrath, forever-and-on, unquenched desire,
brimstone paradise. I've turned a believer of
sorts after all, turncoat, traitor to what I have
arduously taught myself: don't cast me out,
don't ever leave me, desire unquenchable, as
long as he loves me I'm saved.

I'm setting the kitchen timer for half an
hour. It'll be 3 P.M. then, I'll get immersed in the
new account then, a fat folder to be studied, I'll
plot my strategy. In the meantime I'll type. The
story a woman told me, how she lived with a
man for the year it took her to write her first
book, how at 11 P.M. every night he'd turn the
TV up and say, "When will you be done with
your typing?" She became adept at recognizing
the split second when she had to stop—
somewhere between 2 and 3 A.M.—just preced-
ing the moment when he'd start hurling chairs,
books, bottles.

Typing. Recalling in print, pressing wobbly
black buttons. A more or less faithful machine
recording a process: what he makes happen.
The sleepy slave who, at dawn, sits at her
master's feet and recounts in a lullaby voice, a
soothing singsong, what has happened to her
that night, as the sky lightens and before they
go to sleep, endlessly weary, limbs afloat.

Rapidly, too—55 wpm? Not that fast. Could

I play his secretary, give up this lovely, absurd job of mine, be with him around the clock? Beverly, the friendly voice answering his phone: "...may be out to lunch, if he is...message?" From Queens, he explains, "they get paid more in Manhattan, how else are you going to get them out of Queens," my brain registering feebly but of course I say nothing because my stomach surrenders under the blatant, indolent tone of his voice as he says, "You've got to pay those girls more, of course, how else...."; my stomach and thighs responding: faceless girls out of Queens or wherever, just like me, I'm one of them. But ME he loves, ME he allows to bury a face in his armpit, for ME he lights a cigarette with carefully squinted eyes, puts it between my lips, my mouth slightly open, waiting for what he'll put into it next. Tongue, a dribble of wine, cock, a thumb, one square of bitter chocolate, two fingers, four, half a sautéed mushroom, tongue, cock again. For ME he puts a lit Camel between open lips, I make it glow in the dark, our damp thighs stick together while he says, in a low, lazy voice, "How else are you going to get the Beverlys out of Queens?"

Fifteen more minutes before I have to work. Set up by him as surely as if he knew what I need to do, which he doesn't, not in detail. "If you're not getting things done..." Sweet, slow cramp of surrender in my stomach, warm syrup thighs. Yesterday, as we finish dinner at this table, a child sings a nonsense ballad from a nearby window: boisterous, off-key, cheerful. I shout, "Who's the noisy brat." He laughs. He likes it when I raise my voice, he does it so rarely. The singing child didn't hear me. ANYTHING FOREIGN TO OR OUT OF KEEPING WITH A SPECIFIED EPOCH. The epoch's a midsummer in the seventies. The out-of-keeping is me.

BY THE TIME the utter predictability of my orgasm sank into my brain, it had, of course, long been familiar to my body. There was no mistaking the power this man had over me. Like a well-made windup toy, whenever he set me in motion I came. Moods of wanting or not wanting to make love were moods I remembered as from a book. It was not a matter of insatiability but one of inevitability of response. He did what he did and then I always, inevitably, finally came. Only the preludes varied.

I'M HURRYING BACK from the wash-room, where I've hastily brushed my hair, washed my hands, put on lip gloss. Walking rapidly around the corner and down the hall toward my office, I hear a colleague answer the night line. It is six-fifteen, a four o'clock meeting has lasted until a couple of minutes ago. Just as I reach my desk, ready to pick up my briefcase and leave, my phone begins to ring. "For you, love," says a cheerful voice— we've made a good friendship out of a chance bond formed seven years ago, when we both started working here on the same day. There's a click and the outside line is open. "Let's go, time to get out of there, the Chelsea, room ..." "I don't even know where it is," I say. "What's the matter, you just surfaced at Penn Station?" "I've been in this city as long as you have," I say. "I know, sweetheart. Trouble is, you can't ever find your way around in it." "I can too find my way around," I say. "There's no need for me to know where every sleazy little hotel ..." I am bent over my desk, hair shadowing my face at either side like horse blinders. I'm holding the receiver in my left hand while the pencil in my right cross-stitches slowly and carefully around HOTEL CHELSEA, scrawled on the cardboard back of a notepad; the oval wreath consisting of precise, tiny *x*'s completed, I trace the verticals on the *H*, up and down, up, down again, smiling fixedly, his voice skipping on, "... never heard ... stayed there? ... every New Yorker ... a landmark. Half an hour."

The cab driver has never heard of a Hotel Chelsea. He finds it with the help of a tattered collection of pages no longer held together by a cover, sporadically soaked with grease, smudged so thoroughly that I'm impressed by how quickly he deciphers the print. It is not a long ride.

The small lobby is cluttered with unmatched furniture, the walls covered with dusty paintings all done, it seems, during the last two decades. The only occupant besides me and a man behind a counter at the far end of the room is a woman who sits on a vinyl-cushioned black bench placed at right angles to a fireplace. Her deeply grooved face is a mask on a head so small as to appear shrunken. The high heels of her low-cut shoes are dusted with green glitter. Rolled-down argyle socks expose white calves, elegantly shaped as those of an adolescent dancer; what looks like a soldier's dog tag hangs suspended on a shoestring against the Knicks T-shirt tucked into the waist of a salt and pepper tweed skirt. She is reading a Spiderman comic book; *Birds of South America*, a fat library book, lies on her lap. I regretfully stop myself from staring.

The elevator is small, the hallway into which it releases me bleak. I lean cautiously over the ornate, wrought-iron banister. Rows after rows of railing plunge below, the shaft bottomless in the dim light. I pull back sharply, annoyed with myself. Of course it's a long way down, I tell myself, it's twelve floors. ... Though I try to walk lightly I'm unable to keep the heels of my sandals from clicking loudly on the stone floor. When I have found the right room I take a deep breath, glad to close a door against the silence and the gaping stairwell outside.

This time there are no packages heaped on the bed, there is no note. Six dime-store hooks, the size I buy to hang my most lightweight mementos, sit like bugs at irregular intervals on walls that need painting. The squares of white beneath the hooks make the surrounding wall space look even grayer and give the room an air of having recently been evacuated—a place where someone lived, hastily abandoned, no

time to pack, cheaply framed family photo-
graphs hurriedly snatched off walls. A dead
cockroach lies next to the cold water faucet on
the back ledge of the bathroom sink, a smaller
one near the bathtub drain.

I sit down on the orange chenille covering
the single bed and cause the mattress to sag
abruptly. I lean my briefcase against my calf
and do not take the shoulder strap off my right
arm but clutch my handbag under my elbow
and hold on to the strap, my left arm crossed
diagonally over my chest.

The phone finally rings. "Take your clothes
off," he says. "There's a scarf in the top drawer,
tie it over your eyes." The large square—
loosely woven white cotton with a narrow
border of small, pink flowers; a present from
two of my friends three birthdays ago—lies
neatly folded in the left front corner of the
drawer. I take off my dark blue T-shirt and
linen pants, unused to the process of drawing
clothes over my body with my own hands.

The door opens. He locks it behind him and
leans against it, his arms folded. I feel my smile
freeze, thaw, fade in rapid succession. He takes
the three steps to the bed, yanks bedspread and
top sheet together out of my hands, off my
body, off the bed, slaps me so I fall over
sideways, sprawling. I am momentarily disoriented. "Don't cry now," he says, his voice

bland. "There'll be plenty later. It was a simple enough thing to ask you to do."

"This is a creepy room," I say. "I couldn't stand not being able to see, alone in here." "You can't stand much of anything," he says. "Not a whole lot's likely to happen to you, with me right outside." "I didn't know you were...." "Just do it," he says. "I'm tired of talking."

I fold the scarf and tie it clumsily at the back of my head. He sticks a finger between scarf and eyebrow, two more fingers; unties the scarf, redoes it himself. I can no longer see the slit of light along its lower edge. There is a rustle of cellophane, a small paper tear, the click of his lighter, a cigarette in my mouth. He curls the fingers of my left hand into the shape required to hold a small ashtray—it feels like glass. When I have smoked two cigarettes I clear my throat, open my mouth—but there is a knock at the door. I hear his footsteps on the wood floor, the lock being opened, low voices. The second one is as deep as his, but different in quality—a woman's? "About time..." he says, then some mumbling I can't make out, "All right, then..." and, "...Start now."

During the following ten minutes I am being dressed again—by a woman, I'm certain now: her breasts keep brushing against me, they feel soft and large. There is the persistent smell of a perfume I can't identify: not cloying, though sweet; not really sultry, though with an unmistakable hint of musk, and there's some verbena, too. She has long nails, she is shorter than I am, she has recently drunk a small amount of whiskey and has rinsed her mouth with Lavoris. She has coarse hair, quite a bit of it; her hair, like her breasts, keeps touching my skin.

I try to visualize the clothes she is putting on me. The underpants are small, made of slippery fabric, the border scratchy just above my pubic hair. She puts my feet, then my calves, into boots that zip up the inside. The slant at which they support my arches must mean that they have high heels and thick platform soles. A skirt is slipped over my head, zipped in the back. I move the material between thumb and forefinger: it is cold and slippery like a plastic-coated slicker—vinyl: I am wearing a vinyl skirt that ends—my arms hanging by my sides—at the level of my fingertips. A brassiere next. "Lean forward, honey," says the smoker's voice in a conspiratorial, girl-talk tone. "Let's make the best of things here." I bend from the waist while she adjusts my breasts, taking each into the palm of one hand, squeezing toward the middle, pushing the pillows of padding underneath and toward the underarm side of each breast. When she bids me straighten up I run my fingers over what protrudes above the stiff lace: my breasts touch, something they normally do only under the hands of a man. The thought of my breasts so extravagantly positioned makes me giggle. "What's funny now?" he says. "Look," I say. "Put yourself in my place. You're in a hotel, blindfolded, and someone you don't know shovels you into a push-up bra that you'd have given your eye teeth for between twelve and eighteen, except your mother would never let you wear one. You picture that and then tell me if it wouldn't make you laugh." He says, "I see your point."

A top of some sort has been pulled over my head in the meantime. It has no sleeves, ends two inches above the waist and begins where my breasts take cover under rigid lace. A vinyl miniskirt, I think, a top with me hanging out all over it, platform boots: I'm wearing a hooker outfit.

There is no time to interpret this newly solved puzzle. The scarf is off my eyes. Before me in the fading northern light shimmers an enormous, white-blond Dolly Parton wig over heavily made-up eyes, a glossy, dark brown mouth. And there's a black, see-through top, cut low over large breasts in a black lace bra; a purple vinyl skirt ending above mid-thigh, patent leather boots—my twin: two of us in look-alike costumes, contenders in an as yet mysterious contest. I stare.

Neither of the others moves. Only when I sit down on the creaking bed—at last beginning to formulate a question—does he say, "Do the rest."

The rest, taking nearly half an hour, is a wig like hers and a generous application of makeup, pots and tubes and brushes surfacing in turn from a gold lamé kit kept in the bowels of a very large handbag. Though she tries, patiently and with perseverance, she does not succeed in gluing false eyelashes to my lids. I'm not used to the procedure and am unable to keep my eyelids from fluttering hysterically. Instead, she covers my lashes with gobs of mascara, letting one layer dry—fussing with iridescent green eye shadow in the meantime—then applying yet another layer, and another. She outlines my lips with a hard, short pencil, digging in roughly; fills the space so bordered with her dark brown lipstick, then covers everything with a slab of Vaseline. A few more pats and stabs at my wig with an outsize rattail comb and she says, pleased with herself, "Time to check yourself out, honey, mirror's over there." I look at him. He is sitting in the one armchair, an ankle crossed above the knee, his hands in his pockets. He says nothing. I walk slowly to the bathroom door and its mirror, a narrow, diagonal crack marking a right triangle off the top left corner.

It is a sight from which one averts one's eyes if in the company of a man, which one looks up and down quickly and surreptitiously if unobserved and by oneself: an Eighth Avenue prostitute; not a charming Lady of the Night in a Parisian café out of *Irma la Douce*, but a gawky, atrociously painted New York street whore of the seventies, in her cheap wig and come-on sixties gear, as ready to service a john as rob him of his wallet; the woman who shields her face with a large plastic handbag on footage of yet another vice squad roundup on the six o'clock evening news.

I turn back toward the others... can't even bolt and leave, I think, not like this... three people looking at each other in a forlorn little room: twin hookers and a clean-shaven man at ease in a dark blue pin-striped suit, a crisp pale pink shirt, a dark blue tie with small white dots. "You look terrific, honey," says one hooker to another. "I'm not paying you to talk," says the man in the armchair, pleasantly. "Don't you like how she looks?" the hooker persists. "Isn't this just what you wanted?" "You didn't do it for kicks," he says, still amiably. "And that outfit didn't cost you a third of what you charged me." "It's hard matching a costume thread by thread, a little size problem here too, let me tell you...." "Everybody's in a chatty mood tonight except me," says the man. "Take my clothes off. And take your time tonight, we've got plenty of time, that one can use a few hints from a pro. Come over here, sit down, watch. There's a lot you can learn."

I am rooted to the worn spot on the floor before the bathroom. She has begun to undress him—I have never so much as opened a button on his shirt—casually and efficiently, a mother undressing a small boy for his bath, the child too tired from a day outdoors to do anything but stand quietly, she anxious to get his spattered clothes off and him into the water and pajamas then and bed.

When he is lying on his back he says—not looking at me but at the woman standing by his side—"Get your ass over here and into that chair so I won't have to go get you." In a trance I cross the room and sit down. In a trance I watch her climb onto the sagging bed, in a trance I watch her kneel between his legs. I can't keep from trembling though I press my legs together, my elbows on my knees, knuckles jammed against my upper teeth. Her skirt sticks out stiffly, exposing the black triangle of her underpants and her rear. For some seconds I can think of nothing but how flawless her skin is, my brain commenting objectively and in polite surprise at how graceful a collection of shapes such large buttocks add up to; the wig, pompous yellow curls now tucked back and puffed up in a heap between her shoulder blades, hovers where his legs meet. There are only sucking noises first, later he inhales sharply, then there's a moan. It is a sound I know well. It is a sound I have imagined belongs to me—based on what, I think, based on what—could be made audible only by my mouth, was worth a prizewinning lottery ticket, a promotion, all my talent and skill... my fists have turned slippery gray with diluted mascara. Her hand is between his legs, her head moves vertically in long, slow strokes. "That's it...." he whispers and, "Jesus..." There is a scouring pad of yellow steel wool in my fist now, the whole nest gives way under my pull, I fling it behind me, both my hands closing in on her soft, light brown hair, heavily streaked with gray. "What the..." She scrambles up; blurred bodies next and then he is sitting on the edge of the bed. I am bent over his left thigh, his right leg braced across the back of my knees, his left hand clamped around my wrists pinned to the small of my back. He pushes the crackling vinyl back, says, "Hand me my belt," slides his fingers between the elastic and my skin and pulls the scratchy-hemmed underpants down to the top of my thighs.

I grit my teeth in blind terror and a fury new to me. I will not, will not, he can beat me forever, I will not make a sound. . . . A teacher in second grade, saying to a pupil—a sullen boy, larger and taller than the rest of us—when he dropped a pencil and often when nothing had happened at all, "Your father should take you across his knees and pull down your pants and give you what for." Said in a light voice, ominous as a nightmare in its sweetness; once a week an uneasy wave of titters set off to lap across a hushed room, twenty-eight seven-year-olds bending their heads over their desks with a shame as inexplicable to them as it was pervasive. I haven't thought of this teacher or the proximity of moist swamps she conjured up since being released into the care of gruff Miss Lindlay and third grade. And here it is, revived and let loose, vile: more debasing than anything he's done to me in the past, the enforced flesh-on-flesh intimacy far worse than being tied to a bed, than cowering on a floor, handcuffs and chains a kindness compared to hanging like this, buttocks as if served up, blood roaring in my ears. . . .

I do, of course, cry out eventually. He stops but does not let me go. A cool palm gently soothes my skin, fingers tracing lines this way and that; a flat hand moves softly down my thighs to where his legs hold them fast, follows the line between the thighs upward from the knees, back down again, another slow ascent.

"Give me that Vaseline you had," he says, "and hold her hands." My buttocks are being spread, there is the pressure of his finger in my anus, a hand between my legs, one slippery finger sliding easily into place between closed lips. I tense every muscle. I concentrate on yellow spirals whirling against black on the inside of my squeezed-shut eyelids, I grind my teeth, I dig my nails into my palms, more frantic now than when he first started hitting me: I can't bear it, not like this, please don't let me ... my body beginning to move under the slow pressure that urges me to arch against it, soon squirming greedily on his hand. "You think you know what you want, sweetheart"—his low voice in my ear, almost a whisper—"but you go by what your cunt wants, every time," and a fierce blow. "Shut her up," he says, my mouth covered by a perfumed hand into which I bite as hard as I can, the scarf stuffed between my teeth then and held there firmly by someone breathing heavily to my right; and my mouth free again, his hands fondling me until my body succumbs, much more quickly this time, "Please, I can't stand it, please make me come" changing under another blow to a mere "Please...." My body thrown on the bed, the sobbing under a pillow muffled and distant even to myself, a tongue on me and the pillow off and his face above me but the tongue still there, below, quickly making me wail; my head on his shoulder as he stretches full length beside me, his arm around me tightly, his fingers over my mouth, she rides him sitting astride. Across a narrow space she and I watch each other while he comes.

I AM SITTING in a corner seat on the AA. It's only been two months, a little over nine weeks, I've been out of control for two months. A boy sits across from me, curly hair falling over a round forehead, shirt unbuttoned, an open book held rigidly in both hands. I look at him steadily, my body is liquid, afloat. He stares back, twice he's tried to smile. My hands are folded in my lap, one open palm inside another. I don't smile. I am conscious of my new power and the boy across the aisle is, too. Surely not a new power, ancient probably, I just never knew about it; abandon.

At West Fourth Street I get off. The boy cranes his neck, opens his mouth when I look back at him, jumps up in a sudden, awkward rush, but the doors have closed.

The kid in the subway felt it, secondhand. It must seep from my pores. For the past two months I've been in the process of being taught about myself, something new every night, the undercurrent getting stronger by the hour; hands pinned down above my head, shallow gasps, "This is new" ticking in my brain. A conscious new power: vulnerability, perverse if only because it is total, natural as grass nonetheless, or asphalt in New York. Abandon. Take me, anything, do it to me, anything, take me, anything, kill me if it pleases you. But try tying me down, first. Look at me, my eyes closed, your fingers outlined on my cheek, damp hair lying where gravity makes it land as my head falls back against the pillow. Better yet, talk about striking me first, in a low voice, and handcuff me to the table leg and feed me, crouching low. Make me eat you between a mouthful of baked cod and one of home-fried potatoes, first, slowly tipping the glass of wine against my lips until the liquid flows onto my tongue, my eyes closed, you have to gauge how far the glass needs to be tipped, I'm not accountable. Wine dribbling down my chin, no one wiping it off, first, and God surely knows what next: thick welts and a stifled scream for the first time. Tracing the welts, watching your cock grow hard again, watching you trace the welts, feeling your cock grow hard again, our eyes locked.

Weeks later, stifling is no longer possible. Maybe later yet a trickle of blood, what would it feel like to be struck so that one bleeds? When

---

you're four you can't fathom what it's like to be five. If you've never screamed, out of control, you can't imagine how it feels. Now I know how it feels, it's like coming. There is a sound, far away, having to do with me and surely not having to do with me, no responsibility. My body giving up, giving in. No bounds. Foreign sounds far away, I'm not accountable.

Years of intermittent faking behind me. The power to fake ecstasy, the stingy, pathetic control it provides, pantpantpant, ah, darling. "Dynamite in bed," whispers a man to his best friend as I'm about to enter the living room, only a few years ago. I never once came with that man, not in ten months of tireless gyrations, yet he was happy with my responses. Watching him above me as I panted while he came, his eyes squinted shut, red face far above me, I'm in control. No more. This one has taken me on, taken me in, taken me over, he can have it all, how welcome he is to me.

Beyond all limits is the title of a porn flick on Broadway and Forty-fourth. Beyond-all-limits, what a lovely sound, he's promised we'll see it. "We'll go to lots of movies," he says, "once we ride this out, this—phase we're in." He's right. One needs to ride out a phase such as this one. Vision's too blurred, dangerously drunk driving on steep, narrow, winding roads, using them as if the New York State Thruway, going 110, oblivious to drunkenness and speed limits. He's moving me, edging me, step by careful step—nothing drunken about it—there goes one limit, another one, limits falling by the wayside. I'm afloat. After three days, I've gone beyond my limits. For two months now, I've been out of control. Long ago I've lost count of how often I've come, how often I've said, please, don't, please, ah, don't. I beg every night, lovely to beg. "Please what," he says in a low voice and makes me come again, my voice far away, not my voice at all. I plead every night, ugly rasping from my throat, my stomach liquid, warm syrup thighs, out of control.

Listen holy-Virgin-Mary, I'm like you now; there's no need for my control, he's doing it all, he'll do it until he kills me. Can't, won't kill me, though, we're both too selfish for that. So many ways to edge on further, a lifetime full. Thick welts and a stifled scream for the first time, I've been with him only nine weeks and we've long moved beyond stifled screams. The things people do before they need to be killed must be legion. A trickle of blood for the first time—legion. And the reminder: if you do kill me, you'll have to find someone else and is it easy to find women like me?

THAT NIGHT A trickle of blood stained his sheets. He ran a finger through it, tasted it, then smeared the last drops across my mouth and watched the blood dry on my lips while stroking the sweat-wet hair above my forehead. "You really do crave this," he said. "You're as obsessed with it as I am. Sometimes during the day I get the most persistent hard-on, imagining how far we'll go." He slowly rubbed at the crusty flakes around my mouth with his thumb. "Other times I'm frightened. . . ." He laughed. "Hey, there's some pie left over from dinner. Let's eat it and go to bed, it's two o'clock, you're impossible in the morning when you don't get enough sleep."

Next day, after breakfast and while brushing my teeth, I began to cry. He called, "Ready?" and, "Let's go, sweetheart, it's twenty of." A few minutes later he came into the bathroom and set his briefcase down on the toilet seat. He took the toothbrush out of my hand and dried my face, and said, "You have a meeting at nine-thirty, remember?" and, "What on earth is the matter?" He kissed me on both cheeks, looped my handbag over my shoulder, picked up his briefcase, and took my hand. He locked the apartment door while I cried and we walked to the subway while I cried and at one point he said, "Do you have your sunglasses with you?" He took them from the outside pocket of my handbag himself and stuck them onto my nose, fumbling with one of the side bars, unable to find my right ear.

When we got off the subway I was still crying. I cried up the first set of stairs and then up the second set. Within a few yards of the exit turnstiles he threw up his hands and pivoted me toward the other side of the platform and downstairs again and into the subway and up the elevator and into the living room, where he half-pushed me onto the sofa and shouted, "Will you please talk to me," and, "What the hell is going on?"

I didn't know what was going on. All I knew was I couldn't stop crying. When I was still crying at six o'clock he took me to a hospital; I was given sedation and after a while the crying stopped. The next day I began a period of treatment that lasted some months.

I never saw him again.

When my skin had gone back to its even tone

I slept with another man and discovered, my hands lying awkwardly on the sheet at either side of me, that I had forgotten what to do with them. I'm responsible and an adult again, full time. What remains is that my sensation thermostat has been thrown out of whack: it's been years and sometimes I wonder whether my body will ever again register above luke-warm.